*To Luke:
A Wonderful Storyteller!*

Table of Contents

Preface   7

Proper 13   11
Pentecost 11
Ordinary Time 18
    I Fill the Hungry with Good Things
    Luke 12:13-21

Proper 14   17
Pentecost 12
Ordinary Time 19
    I Give You the Kingdom
    Luke 12:32-40

Proper 15   25
Pentecost 13
Ordinary Time 20
    I Have a Plan for Your Life
    Luke 12:49-56

Proper 16   33
Pentecost 14
Ordinary Time 21
    I Lift Up the Lowly
    Luke 13:10-17

Proper 17   41
Pentecost 15
Ordinary Time 22
    Upside-Down World
    Luke 14:1, 7-14

Proper 18 49
Pentecost 16
Ordinary Time 23
  Discipleship Begins in Our Ears
  Luke 14:25-33

Proper 19 57
Pentecost 17
Ordinary Time 24
  Lost and Found
  Luke 15:1-10

Proper 20 65
Pentecost 18
Ordinary Time 25
  That to Which Your Heart Clings
  Luke 16:1-13

Proper 21 73
Pentecost 19
Ordinary Time 26
  Jesus Turns the World Upside Down
  Luke 16:19-31

Proper 22 81
Pentecost 20
Ordinary Time 27
  Jesus Our Teacher
  Luke 17:5-10

If You Like This Book... 89

Preface

These sermons on Luke's gospel are shaped primarily in story form. In the 1970s I taught systematic theology at Wartburg Theological Seminary in Dubuque, Iowa. During that decade a series of books under the title, *New Theology* was published. One of those books was on the re-emergence of storytelling in the theological enterprise. I was deeply intrigued by this old/new idea. I first applied this new learning to the task of preaching. This resulted in one of my first books, *Telling the Story: Variety and Imagination in Preaching*. In that book I explored three basic types of preaching: Didactic Preaching, Proclamatory Preaching, and Story Preaching. My investigation of the relationship between storytelling and preaching had begun!

About a decade later I wrote a second book wholly focused on storytelling and preaching called *Thinking in Story: Preaching in a Post-Literate Age*. I had moved from the thesis that sermons could make good use of story to the proposal that we needed to "think in story" in order to put our sermons together. I had been taught in seminary to "think in idea" as sermon creation.

It was about that time that a new wave of biblical interpretation called "Narrative Criticism" became popular. What attracted me to this field was that scholars were taking much more seriously the story arc of the gospels and other biblical literature. In this way of thinking, a story in a given gospel never stands alone! But that's just what we have been doing for hundreds of years. A pericope in story form is assigned and we focus entirely on that single story for our sermon without grasping the place of that story in the overall structure of the gospel. This was the background for the next series of books that I wrote on preaching the synoptic gospels. In these books I tried, with the wonderful help of narrative scripture interpreters, to show how a given pericope might be yoked in a sermon with other stories in the same gospel. In writing the sermons in *Preaching Luke's Gospel: A Narrative Approach*, I have often used my own advice in the Luke book in formulating my sermon. Oftentimes I couple the assigned Lukan story with another story or stories from Luke's gospel.

Many of the stories told in Luke's gospel seem to be related to Mary's song in Luke 1:46-55. There are in particular many stories told by Jesus that appear to be inspired by Mary's song. I refer in particular to verses 52-53: "He has brought down the powerful from their thrones, and lifted up the lowly; he has filled the hungry with good things, and sent the rich away empty." It is from these verses, therefore, that I have drawn the title of this book *Filling the Hungry with Good Things*.

I would also like to call attention to the fact that many of my sermons end in first person present tense proclamation language. This was a strong emphasis of mine in teaching future pastors how to preach. I sometimes call this "Speaking for God." Let's say the sermon focuses on the forgiveness of sins. Almost all the sermons I hear on this topic will conclude by giving two or three points about forgiveness. Example: "Forgiveness is from God. Forgiveness is for everybody. Forgiveness is for you." What the hearer gets is information about forgiveness.

I propose that we finish our sermon with proclamation of forgiveness rather than with explanation of forgiveness. To do this we must "speak for God." A simple example: "Jesus is speaking to us through this story today. He says to each and every one of you: I forgive you in the name of God. I forgive each and every one of you in the name of God. My love and my forgiveness shall abide with you forever."

The hearer is called to believe and not just to understand. A personal word of gospel proclamation has been addressed to the hearer. That's all preachers can do in preaching! We can announce forgiveness in Jesus' name and stick it in the ears of our hearers. It is the Holy Spirit's job to take that word of forgiveness and move it from ear to heart. That may be the longest journey on earth!

If you are considering using one or more of these sermons in your preaching cycle, I want to give a couple of words of advice. Quite often in a sermon herein I will tell a story about a given person. Please feel free to tell a comparable story from your own pastoral experience rather than the one I propose. Context is all!

Second, I want to note that these sermons have been written a year or so before you would choose to use one of them in your preaching cycle. It was not possible for me to address these sermons to the living context of your present moment in time. Please feel free to contextualize these sermons to your current life situation.

Finally, I wish you well in your preaching of this wonderful gospel of Luke. Let the good news be heard!

— Richard A. Jensen
Professor of Homiletics, *emeritus*
Lutheran School of Theology at Chicago

Proper 13
Pentecost 11
Ordinary Time 18
Luke 12:13-21

I Fill the Hungry with Good Things

> *Someone in the crowd said to him, "Teacher, tell my brother to divide the family inheritance with me." But he said to him, "Friend, who set me to be a judge or arbitrator over you?" And he said to them, "Take care! Be on your guard against all kinds of greed; for one's life does not consist in the abundance of possessions." Then he told them a parable: "The land of a rich man produced abundantly. And he thought to himself, 'What should I do, for I have no place to store my crops?' Then he said, 'I will do this: I will pull down my barns and build larger ones, and there I will store all my grain and my goods. And I will say to my soul, Soul, you have ample goods laid up for many years; relax, eat, drink, be merry.' " But God said to him, "You fool! This very night your life is being demanded of you. And the things you have prepared, whose will they be?" So it is with those who store up treasures for themselves but are not rich toward God.* — Luke 12:13-21

Anxiety: It's an integral part of every human life. We might even say that we're born anxious and we often die anxious. So what shall we do about our human anxieties? The gospel writer Luke and two singing women offer us helpful wisdom for our human plight.

Hannah's Song

The story of Hannah is told in the first two chapters of the Old Testament book 1 Samuel. Hannah is a woman of deep sorrow. She shares that sorrowful condition with many women in all times. She was unable to bear a child. Her womb was closed. Other women chastised her for her condition. What could she do? She decided to have a talk with priest Eli. She prayed with Eli that God might give her a son. If God would do so, she promised that she would dedicate her son's life to God. Eli watched as Hannah prayed in agony. She seemed so out of control that he thought she must be drunk. Hannah convinced priest Eli that she was not drunk at all. She was simply deep in prayer. Eli blessed Hannah: "Go in peace; the God of Israel grant the petition you have made to him" (1 Samuel 1:17).

And God did so. Hannah became pregnant and gave birth to a son she called Samuel. As soon as he was weaned she brought him to the priest so that her son might remain there forever as a servant of God. She lent her only son Samuel to the Lord forever! And so it was. Samuel was to become a prophet in Israel, and he was called by God to anoint a young boy named David for future kingship.

At the birth of her son, Hannah was overjoyed and sang a great song to the Lord. In one verse of her song she sings: "Those who were full have hired themselves out for bread, but those who were hungry are fat with spoil" (2 Samuel 2:5). In other words, the rich have been turned away and the poor have been lifted up. In verses 7-8 she sings of a similar reversal of roles: "The Lord makes poor and makes rich; he brings low, he also exalts. He raises up the poor from the dust; he lifts the needy from the ash heap, to make them sit with princes."

Hannah's song is a song about great reversals. The closing verses of her song address the king. It appears that she envisions a king who will work such reversals in society. Samuel will anoint the king: David. It appears that Hannah is singing about a messiah in Israel who will put her songs of reversal into practice. The word messiah is a transliteration of the Hebrew word "anoint." David is anointed, he is the messiah. Hannah's song implores the messiah to put down the mighty and lift up the lowly. She envisions a messiah who will fill the hungry with good things.

Mary's Song

In the New Testament we hear another song from another woman whose pregnancy seemed divinely ordained. Her name is Mary. Her story is told in Luke 1. We hear the story every Christmas. An angel appeared to Mary. She was to have a son born of God. She was to call her son, born of the Holy Spirit, Jesus. The son would be holy. He would be a child of God. Imagine what must have gone through this young teenager's brain in response to such an incredible promise of God. It's really hard to imagine. Mary's response to all this holy intervention in her life was to simply say: "Here am I, the servant of the Lord; let it be with me according to your word" (Luke 1:38). Martin Luther called Mary's answer the classic definition of the meaning of faith. She heard the word of God. She believed the word of God. That's what faith does!

In response to this surprising news, Mary, like Hannah, sang a song. In fact her song is very much influenced by Hannah's song. Hear just a couple of lines from Mary's song and compare them with her mother-in-the-faith's song: "He has brought down the powerful from their thrones, and lifted up the lowly; he has filled the hungry with good things, and sent the rich away empty" (Luke 1:52-53).

Mary's song, like that of Hannah, seems to be a description of the task of the messiah. The messiah, Jesus, will put down the mighty from their thrones. He will fill the hungry with good things and send the rich away empty!

Luke 12:13-21

Saint Luke, in his gospel, tells a number of stories about Jesus that deal precisely with these themes. Our text for today is one such example. It's a story of the rich being sent away empty. A man is in the crowd around Jesus. He wants Jesus' help. The man's brother, evidently, has control of the family wealth. He, himself, is concerned that he will be left out of the family inheritance. So he boldly asks Jesus to tell his brother that he must get his fair share of the family wealth.

At first Jesus ignores the man's question. "This is none of my business," Jesus replied. Then he gave the man anxious for family wealth a story. That's typical of Jesus. He loves to tell stories. "Be very careful here," Jesus implores the man. "What you are asking for comes very close to sheer greed. Don't you know that life does not consist of our possessions?"

Jesus then proceeded to tell the man a parable. "There was a rich man," Jesus began, "whose crops were plentiful. He was making money hand over fist. The rich man didn't know what to do with all of his wealth. Finally he decided to tear down all of his barns and build bigger barns in which to store his vast quantities of grain and all of his goods. Then the rich man said to himself: 'I will do this: I will pull down my barns and build larger ones, and there I will store all my grain and my goods. And I will say to my soul, "Soul, you have ample goods laid up for many years; relax, eat and drink, be merry." ' "

I'm sure Jesus paused about here in his story to catch the attention of his questioner. It probably all sounded very good to him. The man might have been thinking that if his brother would divide the inheritance with him he could do just like this man. I can imagine him saying: "I could build bigger barns. I could eat, drink, and be merry. I like this story. Keep talking Jesus."

And Jesus kept talking. "You know what God will say to the man with all the bigger barns? God will say, 'You are a first-class fool. This very night your life is being demanded of you. And the things you have prepared, whose will they be?'" And Jesus concluded: "So it is with those who store up treasures for themselves but are not rich toward God."

Jesus has sent the rich man away empty. Jesus, therefore, has fulfilled the messianic mission as sung by Hannah and Mary. The rich are sent away empty.

Do Not Worry

Hannah and Mary sang about a messiah who would send the rich away empty and fill the hungry with good things. In our first story from Luke we listened to Jesus tell a story about a rich man who was sent away empty. The story of the rich farmer that follows thought he had life made with all his riches is a story about filling the hungry with good things (Luke 12:32-40).

This passage opens with Jesus addressing his disciples. "Do not worry about your life, what you will eat, or about your body, what you will wear. Life is more than food. The body is more than clothing." Then Jesus tells them to look up into the heavens to see the birds fly. They don't sow. They don't reap. In contrast, the rich farmer majored in sowing and reaping and it brought him nothing. The birds just fly and God feeds them. God feeds hungry birds! "Don't you know," Jesus says to his disciples, "that you are of much more value in God's eyes than the birds! If then you are not able to do so small a thing as that, why do you worry about the rest?" (Luke 12:26). In other words, why be anxious? What's the point?

Jesus turns from birds to lilies. Lilies neither toil nor spin. But not even Solomon in all his glory was dressed as well as the lilies. And Jesus says: "... how much more will he clothe you — you of little faith! Don't spend your time being anxious about what you will eat or drink. Stop worrying so much. God watches over the eating habits of all the nations of the world so get over your worrying. What are you to do? Here's what you are to do. Strive for God's kingdom and these things will be given to you as well." God, indeed, fills the hungry with good things.

Human Anxiety

Worry! It's built into us. We worried the first time we felt hungry, and we sent a signal to our mother that it was feeding time. And that was just the beginning of our habitual human anxieties. We worry about the end of life as well. We worry about our human relationships. We worry about our marriages and our families. We worry about our job and whether we will make enough money to support those who are dependent upon us. We worry about our health. We worry about the state of our world today and about our state as well. Anxiety is killing us.

In the midst of this worrying world, in the midst of all our anxieties, Jesus speaks a very simple word to us. "Don't be anxious," Jesus says. "I have come to lift up the lowly. I have come to fill the empty with good things."

Hannah sang: "The Lord makes poor and makes rich; he brings low, he also exalts. He raises up the poor from the dust" (1 Samuel 2:7-8).

Mary sang: "God has lifted up the lowly; he has filled the hungry with good things, and sent the rich away empty" (Luke 1:52-53).

How are we to respond to these wonderful promises of God spoken into the midst of our anxious lives? What do we say when God promises to lift us up and fill us up for all eternity? I propose that we answer Jesus' word with the faith-modeling word of his mother, Mary. We say with Mary, we say in faith, "Let it be to me according to your word."

"Do not be anxious, let it be to me according to your word." That's what we say. That's our proper response of faith.

"Don't worry about your life on earth." That's what Jesus says. "Let it be to me according to your word." That's what we say. That's our proper response of faith.

"I fill the hungry with good things!" Amen.

**Proper 14
Pentecost 12
Ordinary Time 19
Luke 12:32-40**

I Give You the Kingdom

> *Do not be afraid, little flock, for it is your Father's pleasure to give you the kingdom. Sell your possessions, and give alms. Make purses for yourselves that do not wear out, an unfailing treasure in heaven, where no thief comes near and no moth destroys. For where your treasure is, there your heart will be also. Be dressed for action and have your lamps lit; be like those who are waiting for their master to return from the wedding banquet, so that they may open the door for him as soon as he comes and knocks. Blessed are those slaves whom the master finds alert when he comes; truly I tell you, he will fasten his belt and have them sit down to eat, and he will come and serve them. If he comes during the middle of the night, or near dawn, and finds them so, blessed are those slaves. But know this: if the owner of the house had known at what hour the thief was coming, he would not have let his house be broken into. You also must be ready, for the Son of Man is coming at an unexpected hour.* — Luke 12:32-40

Last week's story from Luke 12 ended with a strong imperative command. Jesus told his disciples to strive to enter the kingdom of God (Luke 12:31). This week's text, on the other hand, begins with a strong promise. It's in the very next verse in Luke (Luke 12:32). Here Jesus says to his disciples that they should not be afraid and anxious about the kingdom of God. Why? "Because it is the Father's good pleasure to give you the kingdom." That's the heart of our sermon today. Your heavenly Father has given you the kingdom of God. It's yours; free of charge; pure gift. "I give you the kingdom."

Christian Vocation

Let's look a little closer at the text assigned for this Sunday. It begins, as we have said, with the announcement that God has given us the kingdom. I hope you hear that message loud and clear. This is the good news of Jesus Christ for you. So our task is not to live our lives in such a wonderful way that we might enter God's kingdom. No. We have been made members of God's kingdom. For most of us that first happened in our baptism. God spoke to us through the water that day. God said: "You are my child. You belong to my family now and forever." Again, we don't live lives of service so that we *might* become a kingdom child. No. We live lives of service because we *are* kingdom children. God has made that so!

Martin Luther suggests that in our baptism we are made priests before God and toward our fellow humans. He called this the "priesthood of all believers." Luther probably got this idea from 1 Peter 2:9 where we read: "… you are a chosen race, a royal priesthood, a holy nation, God's own people, in order that you may proclaim the mighty acts of him who called you out of darkness into his marvelous light."

God has not only given us the kingdom. God has called us to be royal priests in this kingdom. What does that mean? How are we to live out this priestly calling? Jesus gives us the answer to this question in today's story. First, Jesus tells us to sell our possessions! That's a tough one, isn't it? Most commentators point out that Jesus spoke these words to the twelve disciples as they walked with him to his death. We hear these words in the quite different context of today. How we personally respond to this command of Jesus is the responsibility of each one of us.

Jesus goes on. He invites us to give alms to the poor. Most importantly he invites us to understand that our response to God's kingdom-loving embrace must be the true treasure of our lives. Where our treasure is, Jesus says, there will our hearts also be. Embraced by God, we embrace others.

Then Jesus tells us a parable that is meant to show us how we kingdom people are meant to live. It's really simple advice. We are to be dressed for action at all times. Jesus addresses this advice to the servants of their master. The master has attended a wonderful wedding banquet. His servants must be ready for his return home. In the language of Jesus' day, they were to keep their lanterns lit in order to be ready for their master's return at any hour of the night. These servants will be blessed by the master on his return from the wedding banquet if their lamps are lit when he arrives home. And when the master comes and the lamps are lit for his arrival, he incredibly serves them their next meal. Anytime the master comes home and finds the servants ready for his arrival, those servants are blessed. Jesus concludes his story with the words: "You must also be ready, for the Son of Man is coming at an unexpected hour."

How do kingdom people live? They are always ready to serve. The kingdom has been given to them. They share what has been given with those in need. Hear two stories about kingdom people who kept their lamps lit in the ordinary stuff of daily life.

Kathryn

First, let me tell you a true story of one of God's priests. Her name is Kathryn. She was born early in the twentieth century. Her religious roots were steeped in Swedish piety. Kathryn seemed to know instinctively that she was baptized into the priesthood of all believers. She never wavered from that faith. This was partly due to her relationships with her sisters and brothers. During the whole course of her adult lifetime her family members spoke together of the meaning of their Christian faith when they were gathered together.

She was faithful in church attendance. She knew her mission in life was to be ready to serve others.

Kathryn had a dream of going to nursing school and becoming a registered nurse. However, that was not realistic given her family circumstances. But she had a lot of practical nursing experience on her own at home. At seventeen, she cared for her mother as she died of cancer. Families in the community who had a family member dying at home called Kathryn to help. She was a living witness to the compassion of Christ and to the hope we have in his resurrection.

During World War II she latched on to an opportunity. The government was interested in training local women to be able to give first aid to others. They had imagined that the war could hit the homeland and trained caregivers would be needed for the task. Kathryn enrolled in the class and was thrilled with the opportunity. She used her "nursing gifts" throughout the rest of her life. She gave loving care to her children. One of her daughters remembers the warm touch of her mother's hand on her forehead in the course of her distress. She made sure her children ate a balanced diet. When the children really got sick she kicked into her nursing mode and warmly cared for them. The day would come when she also cared for her husband who was at death's door for many years. Kathryn was ready to give of herself on many occasions.

At her church she taught children in what was called the "Junior Missionary Society." She taught them about where the church sent missionaries and the nature of the mission. She taught them the names of many of the missionaries who were in service to their faith and to their church. She had a strong global sensitivity that was kept aflame in her heart by the great commission of Jesus Christ to, "go into all the world to preach the gospel."

She was also a good musician and sang in her church choir for years. She and a good friend often sang duets for funerals in her congregation. She was very active in the work of the women of the church. At one point in her life she was elected president of the statewide arm of the church women's missionary society.

One of the most astonishing things about her life was the way she always put others first and herself last. One night six family members were playing the card game of Hearts. Suddenly, Kathryn stopped the game. She wanted to know everyone's score and who was behind. Why? She answered, "So the rest of the players could help them catch up." The men at the table were aghast! But that was Kathryn! She wanted to help the ones who were behind. She almost always put herself last.

Kathryn knew deep in her bones that it was God's good pleasure to give her the kingdom. She had been enlisted into priesthood of all believers and commissioned to be ready to serve others in need. She knew she was a royal priest in the kingdom of God. She did nothing spectacular. She just offered everyday love and service to those in need. Her lamp was always lit for service. That's what Jesus calls for in today's story from Luke. That's what we are called to do as well. Our neighbors are our greatest treasures in life. Where our treasure is, there will our heart be also.

Larry

Hear then another story about one who knew in his bones that it was God's good pleasure to give him the kingdom. His name is Larry. He was a high school basketball coach in a large school. When he arrived in his new town he and his wife went church shopping. They found a mid-size congregation that they liked very much.

A year or so into his new congregation, the pastor led a study of the burgeoning charismatic movement. Who is the Holy Spirit? Should I speak in tongues? How does the work of the Spirit affect my life? These and many other questions were discussed over a few weeks' time. This was all new to Larry. He wasn't sure any of this stuff was relevant for his life but he wanted more. On the day of the last class Larry and others in the group asked for more. The pastor had talked about small groups where the gifts of the spirit were encouraged. "Why can't we have a small group like that?" Larry pleaded.

It wasn't long until the pastor invited those interested to join a small group. Larry was first in line! Six to eight couples formed the new group. The sessions were divided into three parts. First, there was Bible Study. Second, each gave expression to a variety of human needs that required prayer. Third, they prayed. At the end of the prayer, time was left for the movement of the Holy Spirit. A few spoke in tongues. Some interpreted the tongues. That is, they gave in English the meaning of the sometimes meaningless sounds of the tongue speakers. Larry often spoke the meaning of a previous tongue.

It was surprising to the pastor that as these mysterious gifts of the spirit were exercised, the group seemed even more excited about the study of Romans. They spent two or three months on just the first three chapters of Paul's great letter. What they encountered seemed to turn their world upside down. It was the passages about God's amazing grace that seemed to dumbfound them. Take for example Romans 3:21. Paul has just finished a long chapter on the fact that no one is righteous in God's sight under the judgment of the law. Then he writes: "But now apart from the law, the righteousness of God has been disclosed…" It is only in the coming of Jesus that humankind can hear the good news that God loves sinful beings and enfolds them into God's kingdom. Just about everyone in the group was stupefied by this strong assertion of "grace alone." It was as if they were reborn as children of God's amazing grace. Church people all, they had never really understood the radical reach, the radical inclusiveness of God's love.

Larry, for one, was reborn in this process! He knew in his heart that it was God's good pleasure to give him the kingdom. His lamp of service was lit. The first sign of this was the fact that the congregation was going to help start a mission congregation a few miles down the road. The pastor asked everyone to consider helping out this new mission by leaving this congregation and joining the new one. Larry did so immediately. Not only did he join the new congregation, he was elected president. That surprised almost everybody. They had never seen that side of Larry. But president he was and he did a great job.

Larry's life was changed in many ways. It changed his approach to teaching and coaching. He was elected president of the home for seniors not far from the congregation in which he was president. He served as leader of a state-wide athletic organization. You get the point. Larry was a man changed by the gospel. His lamp was lit. He was ready to serve.

Some years later Larry met again with the pastor who had led the Bible Study and the prayer group. Larry admitted to the pastor that he was a bit dumbfounded by the many responsibilities he had undertaken as one of the priesthood of all believers. Larry gave the pastor a simple and powerful answer. "Once you taught me about grace," Larry began, "I knew that I was free to fail. So why not give it my all."

Larry knew deep in his bones that it was God's good pleasure to give him the kingdom. He had been enlisted into the priesthood of all believers and commissioned to be ready to serve others in new and challenging ways. He knew he was a royal priest in the kingdom of God. So his lamp was always lit for service in the everyday stuff of life.

The Royal Priesthood

These stories of quite ordinary people who gave their lives for others is just a way to underscore the practical meaning of today's scripture reading. What are we to do as Christians? What is God's will for our life? How shall we serve our neighbor? The story Jesus told gives a very simple answer to our questions. We are to be dressed for action and have our lamps lit. The example he gives is an example of servants who served their master well. There's nothing fancy here; nothing difficult. Just serve God in everyday life situations. Keep your lamps lit. Be ready to serve.

It is true for everyone in this congregation today that it is God's good pleasure to give you the kingdom. You are called by God to be members of the priesthood of all believers and to serve God in your daily vocations.

It is God's good pleasure to give you the kingdom! You are a royal priest of God. Keep your light of service lit. Be ready to serve others in need at all times. Your neighbors ought to be your greatest treasure in life. Where your treasure is, there will your heart be also.

And one more thing. Remember what Larry said. "You cannot fail." God's all-embracing love for sinners will always lift you up and send you on your path to service one more time. God's promise holds true, "I give you the kingdom." Amen.

Proper 15
Pentecost 13
Ordinary Time 20
Luke 12:49-56

I Have a Plan for Your Life

> *I came to bring fire to the earth, and how I wish it were already kindled! I have a baptism with which to be baptized, and what stress I am under until it is completed! Do you think that I have come to bring peace to the earth? No, I tell you, but rather division! From now on five in one household will be divided, three against two and two against three; they will be divided: father against son and son against father, mother against daughter and daughter against mother, mother-in-law against her daughter-in-law and daughter-in-law against mother-in-law. He also said to the crowds, When you see a cloud rising in the west, you immediately say, "It is going to rain"; and so it happens. And when you see the south wind blowing, you say, "There will be scorching heat"; and it happens. You hypocrites! You know how to interpret the appearance of earth and sky, but why do you not know how to interpret the present time?* — Luke 12:49-56

Just about everyone can remember where they were on the morning of September 11, 2001. One man was driving to work and he heard on the radio that people were jumping out of tall buildings in New York City. "What in the world is happening?" he thought to himself. As he continued to listen it all became clear. The United States was reeling from a terrorist attack on our homeland. The Twin Towers had fallen. The Pentagon had been severely damaged. A plane crashed in Pennsylvania. Fear was in the air.

The Sunday after 9/11 the churches in our country were filled with people. We had been shaken out of our complacency. We were frightened. We were worried about our future. "Has God forsaken us?" we seemed to cry. We went to church because we wanted to hear a word from God over our life and over our future. How does all this mayhem fit into God's plan for our lives? Does God have an overall plan for us?

Our text today offers a word of reassurance in response to our pleas. "I have a baptism with which to be baptized…" Jesus says. We'll look into the reality of these words today. We'll see that God does, indeed, have a plan for the whole creation and for each and every one of us.

Old Testament Promise

Let's go back to the very beginning of the Bible. Genesis 1-11 can be thought of as the preamble to the Old Testament story. In Genesis 1-11 we encounter Adam and Eve, Cain and Abel, Noah and the flood, and the Tower of Babel. In the first three of these stories there is a pattern. There is sin. There is God's judgment. There is God's gracious reply. God graciously clothes Adam and Eve even as God ejects them from the garden. God graciously puts a mark on Cain's head even as Cain is sent to be a fugitive in the world. God graciously puts down his bow of war — a rainbow! — so that Noah and his family will know that the flood is over.

When we get to the story of the Tower of Babel in Genesis 11 we expect the same pattern. There is sin: people want to storm the heavens and be equal with God. There is judgment: their languages are confused. But! But, there is no grace here. This pre-history of the people of Israel ends with an open question. Is God's grace at an end? Is judgment God's final word? Does God have a gracious word yet to speak over the future of the human race?

The answer to that question is: Yes. In Genesis 12 God makes a new promise in place of judgment. God gives a new hope of grace to a man called Abraham. God calls Abraham to leave his land, probably present-day Iraq, and set out for a new and promised land. "I will make of you a great nation, and I will bless you, and make your name great... and in you all the families of the earth shall be blessed" (Genesis 12:1-3). There's a new plan for you! There's a new plan for all the families of the earth. God will bless one and all. God certainly has a master plan for all of history and for our individual lives as well.

God's plan goes back almost 4,000 years to the time of Abraham. We need to come to terms with the massive sweep of God's work in the universe. It took God billions of years from the time the universe was put in motion until the time of humans. It took millions more years from the time humans first stepped on the stage of this universe until God called Abraham and offered a promise for all of human life. Think of that! Billions of years. Millions of years. Then God is self-revealed to the human race with a great word of promise. God most certainly has a plan for human life. It is a plan as old as the universe. Jesus Christ will be the great fulfillment of this plan.

This fact about Christianity needs a moment of reflection. Religions come and religions go. Many are born anew in our time. Some men claim that God dictated holy words to them and a new religion was born. Or there is a powerfully spiritual leader who comes up with a new way for people to relate to God. Many people today feel that the Spirit leads them on their own path of spiritual life. New fly-by-night religions are always popping up among us. But it is far better for us to go with the religion that has its roots millions of years ago. We should feel heartened about this news of our Christian faith. It is not a fly-by-night faith. It didn't appear out of nowhere. It is rooted in the very creation of the universe and carried out through men and women called by God and through God's man: Jesus Christ. Indeed, God has a plan for our lives!

God's promise to Abraham is focused on the promise of a new land. In the book of Joshua we read about the fulfillment of this promise some 500 years later. Abraham had journeyed to the new land but it was inhabited by other peoples. It took a few hundred years before the land was in Israel's hands. In Joshua 21:43 we hear these words: "Thus the Lord gave to Israel all the land that he swore to their ancestors that he would give them; and having taken possession of it, they settled there." Promise fulfilled! God's plan is moving forward.

A few hundred years more, around 1000 BC, the kingdom of Israel was formally founded. David was first to be crowned king of all the tribes of Israel. See 2 Samuel 5:1-5. Is that to be the end of the promise/fulfillment scheme in the Bible? We have Abraham. We have David. Is that the end of God's world of promise? By no means! God has another promise in store. This promise is addressed to King David. God said to David:

When your days are fulfilled and you lie down with your ancestors, I will raise up your offspring after you, who shall come forth from your body, and I will establish his kingdom... Your house and your kingdom shall be made sure forever before me; your throne shall be established forever. — Samuel 7:12, 16

Gospel of Luke

This promise, made to David, is the promise of an everlasting king. David was anointed king. The Hebrew word for "anoint" is messiah. To David there is made a new promise. It is the promise of an everlasting messiah. A thousand years later the gospel writer, Luke, immediately connects to this theme in his gospel. In Luke's first chapter the angel Gabriel appears to Mary. The angel says to Mary,

Do not be afraid, Mary, for you have found favor with God. And now, you will conceive in your womb and bear a son, and

> *you will name him Jesus. He will be great, and will be called the Son of the Most High, and the Lord God will give to him the throne of his ancestor David... of his kingdom there will be no end.* — Luke 1:30-33

Jesus is to receive the throne of his ancestor David. He is the everlasting messiah whom God promised to David. Another of God's great promises is fulfilled. God's plan marches on!

In between the prophet Nathan's announcement that David's throne would be occupied forever and Gabriel's announcement to Mary that the son born to her would be David's heir, we hear from the prophet Isaiah. Isaiah had a vision of what the task of the anointed one would be. Listen to the prophet:

> *He was despised and rejected by others; a man of suffering and acquainted with infirmity; and as one from whom others hide their faces he was despised, and we held him of no account. Surely he has borne our infirmities and carried our diseases.... he was wounded for our transgressions, crushed for our iniquities; upon him was the punishment that made us whole, and by his bruises we are healed.* — Isaiah 53:3-5

Isaiah's vision is of a chosen Son of God who will bear our sufferings, heal our sorrows, be wounded for our transgressions, and heal us once and for all. This is an incredibly clear vision of Jesus Christ sung by Isaiah the prophet hundreds of years before Jesus' birth. This is Jesus' destiny. This is what Jesus is "baptized" to do for the human race. That's at least how Jesus puts it in our text for today. "I have a baptism with which to be baptized, and what stress I am under until it is completed" (v. 50). This is the key passage from today's text.

In many passages after this one in Luke's gospel, Jesus speaks of his destiny, of the plan for his life. In Luke 13:33 Jesus speaks of his necessity to be killed outside of Jerusalem.

Jerusalem, he says, is always a city that kills the prophets. So he must be killed. That is God's plan for him.

In Luke 17:25 Jesus says he must push on toward Jerusalem in order to endure much suffering and be rejected by the present generation. When it was all over, Jesus' death and resurrection, women came to his tomb to anoint him for burial. To their great surprise, Jesus was not there! They were deeply perplexed and troubled. What could this mean? Suddenly, two men in dazzling array appeared before the women. "Why do you look for the living among the dead?" (24:5) they say to the women. "Remember how he told you, while he was still in Galilee, that the Son of Man must be handed over to sinners, and be crucified, and on the third day rise again?" (23:6-7). In other words, the dazzling men ask the women if they do not remember the plan that Jesus had laid before them. God had a plan with Jesus. The plan is now complete. Sinners will be pardoned. The sick will be healed. The transgressors will be forgiven. The dead will be raised. That's God's plan with Jesus. That's the baptism with which he had to be baptized.

"I have a plan for your life," the risen Jesus testifies. "I was born, served, died, and rose again and I did it all for you. In the midst of life's many forms of meaninglessness always remember: 'I have a plan for you; a plan of healing and hope; a plan of sin and forgiveness; a plan of death and resurrection.' "

Meaninglessness

We began with 9/11. We began with questions. Has God forsaken us? Will God forsake us in the future? Does God have an overall plan for our lives? These questions raise the overall theme of meaning. Do our lives have meaning in and of themselves? Do our lives have meaning for the future? A dramatic event such as 9/11 can call forth such questions from the depths of our being.

But meaninglessness comes in other forms as well. When life becomes a day-by-day struggle for survival, we wonder about meaning.

Families break apart. We are left alone and in grief. What's the meaning of my life now?

Modern science is unlocking incredible secrets about the functioning of the universe. We are puzzled about the destiny of our universe and of our own destiny. Is there any meaning to it all?

A loved one dies. Is that the end of it? Does death usher us into a formless void? If so, what can possibly be the meaning of life?

Each of you listening today can fill in the blanks here. What is it about life that leaves you puzzled and adrift in the universe? How does this matter of meaninglessness stalk your life?

Is there meaning to life? Does God have an overall plan to rescue and redeem you for all eternity? The simple answer to that question lies in Jesus' word in our text for today. Jesus says, simply, "I have a baptism with which to be baptized..." As we have seen in our walk through scripture today, this baptism to which Jesus refers is the plan of God that goes back billions of years. It starts with the creation of the universe. We think humans first arrived on earth around 3.5 million years ago. About four thousand years ago God set history in motion by making a promise of land, blessing, and nationhood to Abraham. According to the book of Joshua the promise of land was fulfilled around 1200 BC. In 1000 BC a new promise was made to David that his kingdom would live forever. This promise was fulfilled with the birth of the new David, Jesus Christ, to a young woman named Mary. This Jesus said, "I have a baptism to be baptized with... I am the one who comes to bring God's plan to eternal fulfillment. I have an eternal plan for your life!"

Our lives are not meaningless. God has worked for thousands of years to wrap you in God's promise of meaning and purpose for your life. Does my life have meaning and purpose? It most certainly does. It has a purpose launched by God long years ago. The climax of God's plan for us is Jesus Christ. He was baptized for us. His baptism took place on a cross. But Jesus rose from the death that the cross administered. He rose and he speaks to us today. "Don't ever think that your life has no meaning! Your life is anchored in meaning over thousands of years. I have been baptized for you on the cross. I have a plan for your life. You shall live with me forever and ever." Amen.

Proper 16
Pentecost 14
Ordinary Time 21
Luke 13:10-17

I Lift Up the Lowly

> Now he was teaching in one of the synagogues on the sabbath. And just then there appeared a woman with a spirit that had crippled her for eighteen years. She was bent over and was quite unable to stand up straight. When Jesus saw her, he called her over and said, "Woman, you are set free from your ailment." When he laid his hands on her, immediately she stood up straight and began praising God. But the leader of the synagogue, indignant because Jesus had cured on the sabbath, kept saying to the crowd, "There are six days on which work ought to be done; come on those days and be cured, and not on the sabbath day." But the Lord answered him and said, "You hypocrites! Does not each of you on the sabbath untie his ox or his donkey from the manger, and lead it away to give it water? And ought not this woman, a daughter of Abraham whom Satan bound for eighteen long years, be set free from this bondage on the sabbath day?" When he said this, all his opponents were put to shame; and the entire crowd was rejoicing at all the wonderful things that he was doing. — Luke 13:10-17

Whatever Happened to Sin? is a book written by Karl Menninger years ago. He observed in his psychiatric practice that when people poured out their life stories to him, they rarely said anything that sounded like a confession of sin. What is sin anyway? One of the best places to begin a biblical investigation into the nature of sin is with the story of Adam and Eve in the Garden of Eden. Their stories give us a good handle on the very nature of sin.

Eve

The story of these first parents of ours is told in Genesis 3. The first thing we hear in Genesis, the first book of the Bible, is the story of the world's creation. The climax of God's creating is the creation of man and woman: Adam and Eve. Genesis 3 tells us the story of the sin of these parents of ours. At first the story centers on Eve. A serpent appears in the garden. We suspect that this is Satan. Satan asks the first couple if it is true that God had told them not to eat of any tree in the garden. Eve answered, "We may eat of the fruit of the trees in the garden; but God said, 'You shall not eat of the fruit of the tree that is in the middle of the garden, nor shall you touch it, or you shall die'" (Genesis 3:2-3).

Satan roared! "You will not die for God knows that when you eat of it your eyes will be opened, and you will be like God, knowing good and evil" (Genesis 3:4-5). Did you catch the depth of that temptation? "You will be like God. Why live on earth the life of a lowly human when you can be so much more! You can be like God!"

Who could resist such a temptation? Why be simple humans when we could be so much more? Eve, for one, could not resist. She took of the fruit and she ate. Then she gave the fruit to Adam and he ate. Immediately their eyes were opened, and they saw that they were naked and they were ashamed! They surely ought to be ashamed! They have transgressed the basic order of things in this world. They are trying to cross from being human to being "like" God.

We often call this first sin the sin of pride. For centuries the male theologians of the church have spoken of pride as the fundamental way the church understood sin. Pride! I'm not satisfied with being human. I want to be like God. I want to be the center of my own life. I want to be the king or queen of my own domain. I want to be center stage to all that happens around me. I — I — I — I want to be my own kind of god. I want to be the center of my own world. Life will revolve around me! More recently women have begun to take their rightful place as church theologians. They have sought to broaden our definition of sin. It may be a male thing to exude pride. A fundamental sin of females, on the other hand, might be called something like shame or low self-esteem. In the story of Adam this form of sin comes to the fore. (Interestingly, the Genesis story has Eve exemplified as pride-filled and Adam as ashamed of himself.)

Adam

Let's look at the sin of Adam. A few days after the tree in the garden incident, God came walking in the garden at the time of the evening breeze. Adam and Eve didn't know what to do so they hid themselves so that God could not find them. God was puzzled so God called out to Adam: "Where are you?" Adam tumbled out of hiding, ashamed of himself. Adam said to God: "I heard the sound of you in the garden, and I was afraid, because I was naked; and I hid myself" (Genesis 3:9).

"Who told you that you were naked?" God demanded of Adam. "Have you eaten from the tree of which I commanded you not to eat?" Now comes the strange twist of the story. Adam claims his innocence. "It was the woman you gave me, God. She did it. She gave me fruit from the tree. It's not my fault!" Adam is ashamed of himself. If Eve had overweening pride, Adam was filled with shame. His self-esteem was at rock bottom (Genesis 3:11-12).

Adam presents us with a different kind of sinner! Pride is not the problem here. Shame is the problem here. Low self-esteem is the problem here. Adam is ashamed to be in the presence of God. He is guilty and he knows it, but he can't stand up and admit it. He doesn't have enough self-esteem to own up to his own failings.

So two different forms of sin are present in this story: pride and low self-esteem. Perhaps each one of us participates in both forms of sin in our understanding of ourselves in relation to God. Some people think pride is the fundamental sin of males. Low self-esteem, on the other hand, is the fundamental sin of females. It's probably not that simple but these are helpful clues to the meaning of sin in our lives.

The Bent Over Woman

Our story today from Saint Luke is the story of a bent over woman. She might be the poster woman for what some call the fundamental sin of women: low self-esteem. She is a bent over woman! She couldn't stand up straight. She encountered Jesus in the synagogue on a Sabbath day. Teaching in the synagogue on the Sabbath was a normal activity in Jesus' ministry. He was teaching. A woman entered the synagogue. A spirit had crippled her for the past eighteen years. "She was bent over and was quite unable to stand up straight."

Jesus assessed the situation and took pity on this woman in need. "Woman," he said, "you are set free from your ailment" (v. 12). Then Jesus laid his hands on the woman. He did so and immediately she stood up straight and began praising God. So far, so good. But the leader of the synagogue was not happy. In fact he was indignant because Jesus had cured on the Sabbath. He shouted at Jesus: "There are six days on which work ought to be done; come on those days and be cured, and not on the Sabbath day" (v. 14).

Jesus called the synagogue leader a hypocrite. "You would even get water for a needy oxen or donkey on the Sabbath," Jesus replied. Jesus continued: "This woman is a daughter of Abraham!" What more esteem could a person of Jewish origin have in Jesus' day? Jesus went on to say that this woman is bound to be pitied because Satan has bound and crippled her up for these past eighteen years. Jesus really raises the stakes here. Evil is at work in this woman. Evil has left her bound and bent over. Surely Jesus ought to heal such a woman on any day of the week that he wished! It is the Sabbath day to be sure, but Jesus makes it very clear that he is Lord of the Sabbath. Let the healing begin!

Bent Over Lives

Many people among us live bent over lives. Many of us cannot stand tall in God's presence because of our guilt or shame. To use the language from the sin of Adam: many among us suffer from being bent over, from low self-esteem.

Let me tell you of a boy named Johnny. Johnny was not big for his age. He didn't like to play games with the guys at recess time. He stood off by himself. Sometimes he would play games with the girls. Let me tell you that such a life is very difficult to sustain in a masculine culture. So, Johnny was bullied terribly. He didn't know what to do. He couldn't fight back. He could run. He could hide. He could live in shame or he could kill himself! Death seemed to be an easier fate than living in a cultural world where he was not accepted. It happens all the time!

Then there is a bent over woman named Carol. Carol was never the prettiest girl in the class. In fact, she was not very attractive at all. So she felt bent over her whole life. She never measured up. She was never pretty enough. She was not going to marry some prince charming and she didn't. She did marry, however. Her husband had dropped out of high school and lived a life going nowhere. He had no power, no clout in society. So he primarily exercised his power over Carol. He sexually abused her in countless ways. He physically abused her as well. Carol was trapped. She could see no way out of her predicament. Where could she go? Who could she turn to? Her life is hell. She is, indeed, a bent over woman.

One more bent over woman story. Her name is Jackie. Jackie's life was good to her. She had a good mind and received a good high school education. College seemed out of reach for her. Her parents could not afford to help with the costs. She finally found a community college she could attend that wouldn't cost her a fortune. She graduated with good grades and a degree in accounting and then went job hunting. It didn't go well. For nearly two years she searched, she interviewed, she made calls, she took classes. She did all this but still no job. By this time her self-esteem was at an all-time low. Then, out of the blue it seemed, she got an interview and was hired at a pretty good accounting firm with an adequate salary. She was part of a team of accountants with a particular assignment. She found that she did not trust the team system. She had been beaten too low to trust anyone! She felt like her ideas were ignored. If her ideas were rejected, it felt as if she had been rejected. She went to great lengths to protect herself. Two years of job hunting had crippled and left her quite bent over. This also happens all the time.

Lifting the Lowly

Johnny, Carol, and Jackie were bent out of shape. Many of us have bent over parts of our own lives. Our self-esteem can be very low. For us this story today of the bent over woman is filled with good news. Today, Jesus' word to the bent over woman is addressed to us. Jesus' word for all persons feeling bent over in their lives is very simple. "You are free from your ailment," Jesus announces to us. "You are daughters and sons of Abraham. You are daughters and sons of God. You are free to stand up straight. I came to lift up the lowly. I came to free you from the bondage of Satan."

Hear it one more time. It comes right out of Mary's song at the beginning of Luke's gospel. Mary sang of her son about to be born: "He has brought down the powerful from their thrones; and lifted up the lowly." Jesus says to all bent over persons: "I lift up the lowly. I lift you up. I will raise you even to eternal life." Amen.

Proper 17
Pentecost 15
Ordinary Time 22
Luke 14:1, 7-14

Upside-Down World

> *On one occasion when Jesus was going to the house of a leader of the Pharisees to eat a meal on the sabbath, they were watching him closely.... When he noticed how the guests chose the places of honor, he told them a parable. "When you are invited by someone to a wedding banquet, do not sit down at the place of honor, in case someone more distinguished than you has been invited by your host; and the host who invited both of you may come and say to you, 'Give this person your place,' and then in disgrace you would start to take the lowest place. But when you are invited, go and sit down at the lowest place, so that when your host comes, he may say to you, 'Friend, move up higher'; then you will be honored in the presence of all who sit at the table with you. For all who exalt themselves will be humbled, and those who humble themselves will be exalted." He said also to the one who had invited him, "When you give a luncheon or a dinner, do not invite your friends or your brothers or your relatives or rich neighbors, in case they may invite you in return, and you would be repaid. But when you give a banquet, invite the poor, the crippled, the lame, and the blind. And you will be blessed, because they cannot repay you, for you will be repaid at the resurrection of the righteous."* — Luke 14:1, 7-14

A man named George once told a story about the most unusual airplane ride he had ever taken. He had bought his ticket months in advance to assure a seat near the front of the second class cabin. The day came for his flight. His wife dropped him off at the airport. He threaded his way through security showing his ID and obeying every order. And, of course, he took off his shoes. Finally it was boarding time and he stood in line some more. Finally he was ushered to his seat on the aisle in the first row of second-class seats. He was thrilled. And there was no one in the middle seat so he had plenty of room.

After he made himself comfortable he looked around a bit. There seemed to be some kind of problem in the first-class seats. Soon the man who had a very nice first-class seat got up and came back into the second-class section and sat down by George. George was confused. The man who had taken the middle seat saw his confusion and explained the situation. "I'm the president of the airline," he told George. "The man who came to sit where I was sitting had a ticket for the same seat. So I got up immediately and gave him my seat." And George thought to himself: the world is upside down! This never happens. The president of the airline doesn't have to give up his seat to anybody. I don't understand this upside-down world.

Mary

We have regularly been making the point that Mary's song, a song modeled after Hannah's song in the Old Testament, sings the themes of Luke's gospel. Mary sings of an upside-down world and Luke tells endless stories of the manner in which Jesus turns the world upside down. Let's just refresh our memory and hear a couple lines of Mary's song once again.

> He has shown strength with his arm; he has scattered the proud in the thoughts of their hearts. He has brought down the powerful from their thrones, and lifted up the lowly; he has filled the hungry with good things, and sent the rich away empty.
> — Luke 1:51-53

This is an upside-down world to be sure. And Luke tells story after story that carries out this theme. Let's just look at one such story before we come to our reading from Luke for today. Let's look at Luke 7:18-23. Jesus had been going about the land exercising a ministry of healing and forgiveness. We remember that at the beginning of Luke's gospel we heard the story of John the Baptist baptizing Jesus in the wilderness (Luke 3:21-22). John the Baptist, like Jesus, had his disciples too. They had been out on the road observing the ministry of Jesus. They gave a report to their master, John. John was curious about their reports, and he sent two of his disciples to confront Jesus with a simple question: "Are you the one who is to come, or are we to wait for another?" When they ask Jesus if he is the "one to come" they are referring to the Old Testament prophecy of the messiah. "Are you the messiah, Jesus?" That's their question.

Jesus answers their question indirectly. He tells the disciples of John:

> Go and tell John what you have seen and heard: the blind receive their sight, the lame walk, the lepers are cleansed, the deaf hear, the dead are raised, the poor have good news brought to them. And blessed is anyone who takes no offense at me.
> — Luke 7:22-23

It seems that Jesus is telling the disciples that he, Jesus, is busy turning the world upside down. That's what they are to report to John. In other words, John's disciples are to report to John that Jesus is out there serving human need and turning the world upside down. They might also have said to John that Jesus evidently got his commission from his mother, Mary!

Luke 14

Only verses 1 and 7-14 are appointed for our gospel lesson today. But all of Luke 14:1-24 deals with the same topic: the upside-down world. Let's look closely at these wonderful stories of grace. We begin in 14:1 with Jesus' entry into the house of a leader of the Pharisees for an evening meal on the

Sabbath. The Pharisees were dedicated teachers of the law of God as revealed in the Old Testament. As the meal began, a man with dropsy appeared before Jesus. Dropsy is a disease mentioned often from Hippocrates onward. It is symptom of more than a disease. Jesus asks the "lawyers" whether it was all right if he would cure this man on the Sabbath. The Pharisees didn't say a word. They knew very well that healings such as this were not permitted on the Sabbath. So what did Jesus do? He healed the man then and there and sent him on his way.

Jesus then fixed his eyes on the Pharisees and asked them a simple question. He said to them: "If one of you has a child or an ox that has fallen into a well, will you not immediately pull it out on a Sabbath day?" (Luke 14:5). They couldn't or wouldn't reply. But you can bet your last dollar that they wanted to shout, "No!" to Jesus' question. But they stood there in silence. Jesus was turning their world of law upside down.

The two stories that follow in 14:8-11 and 12-14 are first a story about being invited to a banquet, and then about inviting others to your own banquet. Jesus had noticed at the house of the Pharisee how the guests just came in and assumed that the places of honor at the banquet were for them. So he told them a story. "When you are invited by someone to a wedding banquet, do not sit down at the place of honor, in case someone more distinguished than you has been invited by your host; and the host who invited both of you may come and say to you, 'Give this person your place.' " Just think of how humiliating that would be! You come in and take a choice seat and then the party giver boots you out of your seat and directs you to a seat of lesser honor. A little chunk of your personal world has just been turned upside down. You thought too highly of yourself! Shame on you.

Jesus' advice is that when you come to a banquet you should take the seat in the lowest place. The host may then come to you and say, "Friend, move up higher." Jesus continues saying, "For all who exalt themselves will be humbled, and those who humble themselves will be exalted." Jesus turns the world upside down as well.

Then Jesus offers advice to us when we are the ones planning the banquet. We are to follow the same upside-down principle. We are not to invite our friends. We are not to invite our relatives or our rich neighbors. When we act in that way we are simply thinking that the people we invited will invite us back to their next party. Rather, Jesus says, "... when you give a banquet, invite the poor, the crippled, the lame, and the blind. And you will be blessed, because they cannot repay you, for you will be repaid at the resurrection of the righteous" (v. 13). This is an upside-down world to be sure!

The story that follows in Luke 14:15-24 picks up the same theme. One of the dinner guests at the table with Jesus shouts to him a pious phrase. "Blessed is the one who will eat bread in the kingdom of God!" (v. 15). I'm sure the man who uttered these words was pleased with himself. What a pious man he was!

Jesus wasn't buying pious platitudes. He told them another story. A man threw a wonderful dinner party. When it was time to begin, he sent his slave to invite to the party all who had received an invitation. The slave set off to do his job, but he met with a great surprise. The people who had been invited to the party had a thousand reasons why they couldn't come. One had just bought a piece of land and he had to go inspect it. Another had just bought five yoke of oxen and he had to try them out. Another had just gotten married and, of course, he could not come to the party either.

When the owner of the house heard all of the excuses he was livid with anger. In his anger he commanded the slave to go out again into the streets and lanes of the city and bring in the poor, the crippled, the blind, and the lame. The slave replied that he had already done that and many had come but there were still empty seats at the banquet. The master said to the slave, "Go out into the roads and lanes, and compel people to come in, so that my house may be filled. For I tell you, none of those who were invited will taste my dinner" (vv. 23-24). With this stroke the master turned the world upside down. The worthy were sent away. The unworthy were compelled to come in. Luke's gospel makes it abundantly clear over and over again that the God revealed in Jesus has an upside-down way of thinking compared to our normal train of thought. The world that God enfolds through the ministry of Jesus Christ simply turns our normal ways of thinking upside down.

Prestige

We could probably say that gaining prestige for ourselves is the American way of life. Prestige is an important commodity for each and every one of us. It started out when we were children. As kids we soon learned the importance of being somebody! We could gain "somebody" status in a variety of ways. Maybe we were the best looking boy or girl in our class. Or we came from a very wealthy family. That was always impressive. Another way to gain prestige was through our academic achievements. How good it felt to have the teacher and some of the other kids admire us for our brain power! Prowess in athletics was another avenue to prestige. Great ability in the music field was another pathway to prestige.

However we seek or sought prestige as children, our goal was to be noticed by others, to be accepted as a person of worth, to be appreciated for our gifts. We wanted to be the top of our class in something. We wanted to achieve status and prestige for ourselves. It's the core longing of human beings we are talking about here. And when we achieved success in an area of life, we could easily feel that we were on the top of the world looking down on others.

When we become adults seeking to achieve "top of the world" status there are many avenues open to us. We do have our pride after all! We are very interested at times in achieving a high level of prestige for ourselves. We can achieve status for ourselves, for example, by the size of our paycheck. In our country it is assumed that big money means a big person. Or maybe we try to make an impression on others by the size of the house we live in or the flashy new car or truck we just bought. We can be awarded achievement status at work. Some might achieve status and prestige because we are beautiful people or that the person to whom we married is a truly marvelous looking man or woman. Or, we are admired by all for the way we are raising our children or for the accomplishments of our children. In any of these ways and more we can achieve status on the "top of the world" so to speak. It is just a basic human instinct that we want to live on the "top of the world." We want to be on the top looking down. It just feels so good, and it is so fundamentally human.

Jesus

We confront a basic fact here. We long for prestige. We long to be on the top looking down. We long to be honored for our achievements. And then we remind ourselves of the stories from Luke that we have just heard. When you go to a banquet do not take the seat of a high achiever. Take the lowest seat and the hosts may call you to sit in a higher place. When you give a banquet don't invite the prestige people in town. You can do that, of course, and they will invite you back. Your achievement status is kept strong. But Jesus says, "No," to all of this. When you give a banquet invite the poor, the crippled, the lame, and the blind. Then comes

Jesus' punch line: "You will be blessed because they cannot repay you, for you will be repaid at the resurrection of the righteous."

In other words, in God's upside-down world, real status and prestige is not something we achieve. Status and prestige is something we receive from God as a gift. Status in the kingdom of God is not achieved. It is received. It is a gift. And this gift can free us from a world that can hold us in bondage to our need to achieve our own reward. Prestige in the kingdom of God comes through receiving. It does not come through our achieving.

Jesus speaks to us through these stories today. He speaks to us a word of grace. "I see you today in bondage to a world of achievement. I see in you the deep need to be on top of the world. I see in you longing for prestige. I have come to invite you to receive, rather than achieve. I have come to turn everything upside down when it comes to the deep need of human achievement. I have come to invite the poor, the maimed, the lame, and the blind to my banquet. I have come to invite you to my eternal banquet. You are mine. You are mine now and forever. Join me at the top of the world."

There is your prestige! Receive it as a gift. Amen.

**Proper 18
Pentecost 16
Ordinary Time 23
Luke 14:25-33**

Discipleship Begins in Our Ears

> *Now large crowds were traveling with him; and he turned and said to them, "Whoever comes to me and does not hate father and mother, wife and children, brothers and sisters, yes, and even life itself, cannot be my disciple. Whoever does not carry the cross and follow me cannot be my disciple. For which of you, intending to build a tower, does not first sit down and estimate the cost, to see whether he has enough to complete it? Otherwise, when he has laid a foundation and is not able to finish, all who see it will begin to ridicule him, saying, 'This fellow began to build and was not able to finish.' Or what king, going out to wage war against another king, will not sit down first and consider whether he is able with ten thousand to oppose the one who comes against him with twenty thousand? If he cannot, then, while the other is still far away, he sends a delegation and asks for the terms of peace. So therefore, none of you can become my disciple if you do not give up all your possessions."*
> — Luke 14:25-33

Jesus called the twelve disciples. Jesus calls us to be disciples as well. So what does that mean? What does it mean to be a true disciple of Jesus? Images dance in our heads of some we might think of as true disciples. Some of us might remember a visit from a missionary who held us spellbound. Here was a person who had given up her own life to be a missionary in Africa for 35 years. Surely she was a true disciple in every sense of the word.

Others might think of a more local church worker: a pastor, a parish worker, or perhaps a lay member who has contributed greatly to the life of a congregation. We admire such people. We respect such people. Surely they are true disciples.

We not only think of a true disciple as one who works in God's church though it is quite natural for us to start there. We might also think of someone in our own family. Perhaps we think of a good father. We think of this father as one who loves his children with a passion, who shares his gifts with the community, a man looked up to by everyone in the community.

In each of these examples, discipleship is defined in our minds by the deeds of a person's life and that is surely a mark of a great disciple. Our text for today challenges everyone to aspire to serious discipleship. But the final focus of these texts is not what people do to be good disciples. The final focus of the text and its surrounding verses is about what people hear to become good disciples. True discipleship, we learn, always begins in our ears.

The Cost of Discipleship

In today's appointed scripture reading, Jesus is out and about doing his ministry. Large crowds pressed upon him from every side. They had heard about this man. They had heard of his mighty works of healing and exorcism. They were excited by his presence among them and eager perhaps to join the ranks of those who have been ministered to by Jesus. Can you imagine the hope that sprung up in their hearts as they gathered around him?

Then Jesus does something very surprising. He speaks hard words to those gathered. "Whoever comes to me and does not hate father and mother, wife and children, brothers and sisters, yes, even life itself cannot be my disciple" (v. 26). Can you imagine the astonishment that took hold of the crowd? This is not what they came to hear. They came to hear a gentle Jesus who would heal the sick and care for the poor. They came because they wanted something out of

Jesus and Jesus turns it all around. He wants something out of them! He wants them to forsake their families and follow him.

I think we are equally surprised at this turn of events. Jesus' word to the crowds, Jesus' word to us today, is harsh and hard indeed. We are supposed to hate our family in order to follow Jesus? It is important here to remember the life situation of Jesus' followers that Luke was addressing in his gospel. Things were very difficult for the first Christians. They faced much persecution for their faith. It was not at all unheard of that one who chose to believe and follow Jesus was kicked out of their own family. In this context Jesus is issuing a call for people to put him first on their priority list.

Jesus' word could certainly apply to us today as well. Jesus is calling us to make him the number one priority in our lives. Each one of us struggles with this challenge from Jesus. Is Jesus our number one priority? If so, what does that mean for the daily living of our lives? This challenge of Jesus to put him first in our lives is a day-by-day question for us. It is a question that challenges the basic priorities of our lives.

Jesus is not done with hard words. The one who was crucified for us upon a cross calls for us to carry our own cross. "Whoever does not carry the cross and follow me cannot be my disciple" (v. 27). In Luke 9:22 we hear Jesus say to his disciples: "The Son of Man must undergo great suffering, and be rejected by the elders, chief priests, and scribes, and be killed, and on the third day arise." Jesus has determinedly set his face to Jerusalem to bear the cross for us. As he makes his perilous journey to the cross, he invites us to join him in his suffering. He invites us to take up our cross and follow him. He invites us to share in his journey of suffering.

Jesus knows his word is hard for us to hear. He counsels us, therefore, to count the cost of following him. If we fail to count the cost, we might walk on in foolishness. We will be like one who intends to build a tower. The first thing you do to tackle such a project is sit down and count the cost. We need to be sure we can bear the cost of our project. If we do not correctly count the cost, we can be fairly sure that our tower-building task will come to ruin and people will laugh at us. They will ridicule us. "This fellow began to build and was not able to finish," they will whisper. If one is to be a disciple of Jesus, one must first count the cost.

Jesus gives another analogy of the futility of our intent to be a disciple without first counting the cost. "Or what king," Jesus begins, "going out to wage war against another king, will not sit down first and consider whether he is able with ten thousand to oppose the one who comes against him with twenty thousand?" (v. 31). Being a Christian, following Jesus, and taking up our cross is costly business! It could even cost us our lives.

Jesus calls us to be disciples. It's not an easy task that he sets before us. We may need to go against the grain of our own family to be a disciple. We must count the cost carefully if we want to walk in Jesus' footsteps. We must be willing to give up all our possessions in order to follow Jesus. The theme of possessions runs throughout Luke's gospel. We hear it in Mary's song that introduces Jesus' ministry: God sends the rich away empty. Jesus said his ministry was to the poor (Luke 4:18-19). Jesus tells a story about a rich young ruler who could not give away his riches to join God's kingdom. Luke also tells a story about a rich man and a poor man named Lazarus. It was Lazarus, the poor man, who upon his death was carried off by angels to be with Abraham. It was the rich man who wound up in agony in the flames (Luke 16:19-31).

There we have it. Three charges Jesus gives us about discipleship. We may need to leave family behind. We need to count the cost of such discipleship. We need to give up our possessions. It's all quite a challenge and here we need to be very careful about how we understand these threefold tasks of discipleship. It is not the doing of these things that makes us disciples of Jesus. Let me repeat that: it is not the doing of these three things that makes us disciples of Jesus. If it were, we would be right back in the world of good works.

In the world of good works we become acceptable to God because of what we do with our lives. We know in our bones that this way of saying this would stand in radical conflict with other passages in the New Testament. Saint Paul, for example, makes it clear that our good works are not the path to discipleship; our good works do not serve as our qualification for God's kingdom. Listen to Paul from Ephesians 2:8-10: "For by grace you have been saved through faith, and this is not your own doing; it is the gift of God — not the result of works, so that no one may boast. For we are what he has made us, created in Christ Jesus for good works, which God prepared beforehand to be our way of life."

The good works of discipleship are not our own doing says Saint Paul and the entire New Testament. Our good works are created in and through us by the power of the love of God in Jesus Christ. Discipleship, therefore, does not begin in the works of our hands and the sacrifice of our bodies. Discipleship does not begin with us... period! Discipleship begins with what we hear. Discipleship begins in our ears!

That Which We Hear

Following the text appointed for today are two verses that need to be considered in the same context. Jesus says about salt: "Salt is good; but if salt has lost its taste, how can its saltiness be restored?" (14:34). The answer is that bad salt cannot be restored. It should be thrown away, cast on a manure pile! It seems clear that Jesus is still talking about disciples in these verses. There are disciples who are salty. They are good disciples. There are disciples who have lost their saltiness. Here is another warning from Jesus about the cost of discipleship.

Jesus closes this whole dissertation about disciples with a simple saying: "Let anyone with ears to hear listen!" (14:35). There is something about true discipleship that begins in our ears and we are to listen to what we hear.

There are three fundamental instances in our lives as Christians where our ears hear the promises of God. The first instance, at the very beginning of most of our lives, is the word addressed to us in our baptism. Many of us were baptized as children. There, at the very beginning of our Christian walk with God, God spoke to us through the words of a pastor. The words spoken usually begin with a simple announcement. The pastor simply says: "I baptize you in the name of the Father and of the Son and of the Holy Spirit. Child of God, you have been sealed by the Holy Spirit and marked with the cross of Christ forever."

Words like these were spoken over many of us in our infant lives. We heard, if dimly, that we are children of God. We heard, if you will, our call to discipleship. We spend our lives responding to this incredible promise of God. "You are a child of God." That's your call to discipleship. We heard it with our ears. Discipleship begins in our ears!

The church practices baptism as a once-for-all event. We are only baptized once but we come to the Lord's table continually. God speaks to us at this table. The words are simple. "Take, eat, this is my body. Take, drink, this is my blood." That's God speaking to you. That's God putting words in your ears. That's God putting words in your ears continually that you might be constantly renewed as a disciple of Jesus. Discipleship is founded on the promise made to us in our baptism. Discipleship is sustained in us through God's ongoing word at this table. Discipleship begins in our ears. Discipleship is sustained through our ears.

God also speaks to us on an ongoing basis through various kinds of words. God speaks to us through the words of the Bible. God speaks to us through the words of other Christians who reassure us that God loves us. God speaks to us from the pulpits of our churches. Gods speaks and announces to us over and over that we are his, we are loved, and we are disciples. Discipleship is born in our hearing.

The Practice of Discipleship

We are disciples, each and every one of us. We heard it and we continually hear it through our ears. When our ears hear the good news that we are disciples, our eyes open wide to see ever new fields of service.

When our ears hear the good news that we are disciples, our hands reach out to feed the hungry, care for the needy, and care for the children and the elderly.

When our ears hear the good news that we are disciples, our feet carry us to ever new fields of service and mission.

When our ears hear the good news that we are disciples, our mouth testifies to all we meet that they, too, can hear and believe God's promises. We can speak a word of love and grace and acceptance to sinners everywhere.

Discipleship begins in our ears. Discipleship continues in words and deeds of love. Amen.

Proper 19
Pentecost 17
Ordinary Time 24
Luke 15:1-10

Lost and Found

> *Now all the tax collectors and sinners were coming near to listen to him. And the Pharisees and the scribes were grumbling and saying, "This fellow welcomes sinners and eats with them." So he told them this parable: "Which one of you, having a hundred sheep and losing one of them, does not leave the ninety-nine in the wilderness and go after the one that is lost until he finds it? When he has found it, he lays it on his shoulders and rejoices. And when he comes home, he calls together his friends and neighbors, saying to them, 'Rejoice with me, for I have found my sheep that was lost.' Just so, I tell you, there will be more joy in heaven over one sinner who repents than over ninety-nine righteous persons who need no repentance. Or what woman having ten silver coins, if she loses one of them, does not light a lamp, sweep the house, and search carefully until she finds it? When she has found it, she calls together her friends and neighbors, saying, 'Rejoice with me, for I have found the coin that I had lost.' Just so, I tell you, there is joy in the presence of the angels of God over one sinner who repents."*
> — Luke 15:1-10

Did you ever get lost when you were a young person? Not just "play lost" but really lost? It's a frightening experience. One feels so alone and scared. When will this ever end? Will somebody find me? Am I lost forever? Then, seemingly out of nowhere, a hand reaches out to us. Someone has found us. Maybe it was a parent or a brother or a sister or a friend. It really doesn't matter who it was that found us. What matters is that we were found. Being found filled us with tears of joy. We were lost and now we are found!

The Lost Sheep

In our appointed text from Luke for today, Jesus is surrounded by two very different kinds of people: tax collectors and sinners. Neither of these groups of people were part of the "establishment" of that day. Tax collectors are never popular. Sinners are bad people. What's a nice Jesus like this doing surrounded by such an offbeat group of people? That's the question that haunted the upper crust of Jesus' day. That's the question that haunted the Pharisees and the scribes. Here they thought Jesus might have been someone who had come as a special person from God and then he is surrounded with such a lower class of people. They shouted out their disgust: "This fellow welcomes sinners and eats with them" (v. 2). If this Jesus really comes from God surely he would not want to be seen in such lowly company. It's blasphemy.

In response to the Pharisees and scribes, Jesus tells three similar stories. Two of these stories are in our appointed reading for today. The third story, the story of the prodigal son, which is appointed for another Sunday in the church year, carries out the same theme. In the first story it is a sheep that is lost. Concerning the lost sheep Jesus says, "Which of you having a hundred sheep and losing one of them, does not leave the ninety-nine in the wilderness and go after the one that is lost until he finds it? When he has found it, he lays it on his shoulders and rejoices" (vv. 15:4-5). What's the next thing the shepherd does with the sheep that was lost and is found? He calls the whole neighborhood together. We're going to have a party! "Rejoice with me, for I have found my sheep that was lost," the shepherd says (v. 6).

Then Jesus makes a surprising summary statement. He leaps from the sheep that was lost to a profound theological statement: "Just so, I tell you, there will be more joy in heaven over one sinner who repents than over ninety-nine righteous persons who need no repentance" (v. 7). Jesus praises repentance as the very entry into the kingdom of heaven.

But what Jesus calls repentance does not come anywhere near our common understanding of repentance. We usually understand repentance as confession of our sins in order that we might be put right with God. But there is no confession of sins in the stories Jesus tells. None at all. Jesus talks about the lost being found. Repentance, it seems in this story, is about the lost being found. Repentance happens, therefore, when Jesus finds us in our lost human sinfulness. Repentance is not what we do to get into Jesus' kingdom. Not in this story! Repentance, rather, celebrates that we lost sheep have been found by God.

That's why Jesus ate with tax collectors and sinners. He was busying finding the lost, and the lost experienced repentance! They were found. They were found eating and drinking with Jesus. The scribes and Pharisees could not understand this at all. Maybe we have trouble understanding it as well. But there it is. Repentance happens when the lost is found! That's what happened to the sheep. That's what happens to us when God finds us!

The Lost Coin

Just in case the scribes, Pharisees, and perhaps ourselves as well, don't get it, Jesus tells his second story. This story is about a lost coin. A woman had ten coins but lost one of them. Just as the shepherd left the ninety-nine to find the one who was lost, so this woman leaves the nine coins behind and takes a lamp and sweeps the house clean and searches diligently until she finds it. When she finds it, what does she do? Just like the shepherd who found a lost sheep, she throws a party. "Rejoice with me," she tells those invited to her party, "for I have found the coin I had lost." And Jesus adds: "Just so, I tell you, there is joy in the presence of the angels of God over one sinner who repents" (vv. 9-10). And what is repentance in this story? It is the lost coin being found.

Repentance happens when the lost are found. Repentance happens when Jesus finds us.

The Lost Son

Jesus' two stories of the lost being found is followed by one of his most famous stories of all: the story of the prodigal son. "This fellow welcomes sinners and eats with them" (v. 2). That was the complaint of the scribes and Pharisees! Jesus answers their challenge by telling three stories of the lost being found. The prodigal son story is the last in the trilogy of stories that make an incredible assertion: God in Jesus Christ came to find the lost!

This story begins with the fact that there was a man who had two sons. The younger of the sons wanted out of the family. Now! "Just give me my share of the inheritance," he told his father, "and let me out of here." And to a distant country he went. We all kind of know what the distant country is like. It's the place where we waste ourselves. The prodigal certainly went to waste. He spent all of his money. He was destitute. He got the most despicable job a good Jewish boy could ever have. He took care of animals that were considered unclean. He took care of pigs.

One day the prodigal son "came to himself." He was thinking about his plight. He had sunk into the great depths of life. He thought about the home he had left behind. He thought about the fact that the hired men of his father's had a better life than he had. Maybe he could go home! Yes, that's it. Go home. In preparation for going home he polished up a nice prayer to say to his father. His prayer went like this: "Father, I have sinned against heaven and before you; I am no longer worthy to be called your son; treat me like one of your hired hands" (15:18-19). Now that sounds more like our traditional understanding of repentance. The prodigal son would go home and repent. That sounds more like what repentance means!

And maybe it is. The problem is, the Father never gave his son a chance to say his repentance prayer! The father had been watching the roads for any sign of his son's return ever since the son turned his back on father and home. The father was watching! Every day! Watching. Then he saw his son far off in the distance. The father ran to welcome the prodigal home. It was a humiliating run for the father. In ancient Middle Eastern culture men never ran. To run you have to pull up your robes and expose your legs. Awful! Embarrassing! Ugly! But off he ran making a complete fool of himself. (Think of God making a fool of himself as God came in a manger to welcome us home.) When the father in the story reached the son, he did something else that was very embarrassing. He kissed his son. Middle Eastern fathers never kissed their sons in Jesus' day. No way! But the father did it! Why? Because the lost was found.

The father ordered that the lost son be quickly robed, a ring put on his finger, and sandals on his feet. Why? The father says it loudly and clearly: "... this son of mine was dead and is alive again; he was lost and is found!" (15:24). He was lost and is found. The sheep was lost and found. The coin was lost and found. The son was lost and found. Repentance happens when the lost is found!

That's Jesus' answer to the question of the scribes and Pharisees. "This fellow welcomes sinners and eats with them," they complained about Jesus' behavior. Jesus answered: "I eat with sinners because in eating with them the lost is found." The lost is found. That's what these stories teach us about the meaning of repentance. Repentance happens when the lost are found. Repentance happens when God finds us! Repentance happens for us when we accept the reality that God in Jesus Christ has found us.

The Table: A Party for the Lost

These stories about repentance, stories of the lost being found, do upset some of our more traditional ways of thinking about repentance. We often think of repentance as our means of entry into God's presence. First, we repent and then God forgives us. This mindset is often deeply shaped by our experience of Holy Communion. There was a time in some of our churches not so long ago when Holy Communion was served only a few times a year. In some of these churches there were elaborate services of repentance in readying people for communion held the day before the actual communion experience. In other words, we had to get ourselves ready for Holy Communion. We had to repent of our sins. We had to reconcile ourselves with others. Repentance was the human preparation for God's table!

What stood behind this understanding in many instances was a reading of Saint Paul's communion instructions in 1 Corinthians 11. There Saint Paul warns that if we do not properly discern the body as we participate in communion, we are liable to God's judgment (1 Corinthians 11:27). We might get sick and die if we have not properly prepared ourselves for Holy Communion, if we have not properly discerned the body of Christ, or if our repentance is not true! Holy Communion is serious business indeed. The very health of our bodies is at stake here. Proper repentance means everything.

What we have come to realize is that this fixation on the body of Christ that we must be careful to discern is not a proper understanding of what the body of Christ, the bread and wine, really mean. Discerning the body of Christ has more to do with the way in which the members of the body of Christ esteem each other. Paul was concerned about the divisions that existed in the members of the congregation at Corinth. The body of believers was seriously divided. People would only eat and drink with people in their own group.

Some ate way too much while others went hungry. The social divisions in society were carried into the church. Paul wrote to them: "Should I commend you? In this matter I do not commend you!" (1 Corinthians 11:22). When Christians gather together around the body and blood of Christ, they are to gather as one body.

A well-intentioned misunderstanding on this matter has seriously impacted the way many people have thought about Holy Communion over the years. We were sometimes more focused on the nature of the bread and wine than we were on the nature of the community that had gathered. This has led to many problematic practices regarding Holy Communion. Church leaders over the years have turned many people away from the table for fear that their repentance might not be enough to qualify them to eat and drink.

We have heard Jesus tell three stories about the lost being found as the true meaning of repentance. Repentance in these stories is simple: the lost are found. And that's what happens when we celebrate Holy Communion. You are not invited to come to this table because you qualify in some way to be here. You are not invited to this table because you are properly repentant. Not at all! You are invited to come to this table because you are lost in your relationship with God. Here, in the body and blood of his Son, God comes to find you! Repentance, remember, happens when the lost are found! Holy Communion is a place where the lost are found! The shepherd who found the lost sheep threw a party. So does God. The woman who found a lost coin threw a party when the lost was found. So does God. The father who found a lost son threw a party when the lost was found. So does God. God's party is called Holy Communion and God invites all lost ones to come to this table. God speaks to us here. "Take and eat. This is my body. Take and drink. This is my blood." And so we eat and we drink and God fills us with

God's incredible love. And so it happens: The lost are found. You are found. I am found.

There is a very helpful passage in Paul's letter to the Romans. Paul writes: "Do you not realize that God's kindness is meant to lead you to repentance?" (Romans 2:4). Grace leads to repentance. It's not the other way around. It's not that repentance leads to grace. At least that's not the case in the three stories Jesus told. A sheep was found. Repentance! A coin was found. Repentance! A son was found. Repentance! At the table we are found. Repentance!

We sing about this reality all the time in that famous hymn titled, "Amazing Grace."

Amazing Grace how sweet the sound,
That saved a wretch like me.
I once was lost but now I'm found.
'Twas blind but now I see. [repeat!]

Amen.

Proper 20
Pentecost 18
Ordinary Time 25
Luke 16:1-13

That to Which Your Heart Clings

Then Jesus said to the disciples, "There was a rich man who had a manager, and charges were brought to him that this man was squandering his property. So he summoned him and said to him, 'What is this that I hear about you? Give me an accounting of your management, because you cannot be my manager any longer.' Then the manager said to himself, 'What will I do, now that my master is taking the position away from me? I am not strong enough to dig, and I am ashamed to beg. I have decided what to do so that, when I am dismissed as manager, people may welcome me into their homes.' So, summoning his master's debtors one by one, he asked the first, 'How much do you owe my master?' He answered, 'A hundred jugs of olive oil.' He said to him, 'Take your bill, sit down quickly, and make it fifty.' Then he asked another, 'And how much do you owe?' He replied, 'A hundred containers of wheat.' He said to him, 'Take your bill and make it eighty.' And his master commended the dishonest manager because he had acted shrewdly; for the children of this age are more shrewd in dealing with their own generation than are the children of light. And I tell you, make friends for yourselves by means of dishonest wealth so that when it is gone, they may welcome you into the eternal homes. 'Whoever is faithful in a very little is faithful also in much; and whoever is dishonest in a very little is dishonest also in much. If then you have not been faithful with the dishonest wealth, who will entrust to you the true riches? And if you have not been faithful with what belongs to another, who will give you what is your own? No slave can serve two masters; for a slave will either hate the one and love the other, or be devoted to the one and despise the other. You cannot serve God and wealth.'" — Luke 16:1-13

We cling to a lot of things in life. We cling to our loved ones. We cling to our home. We cling to good friends. We cling to our sports heroes and sports teams. The list could go on and on. How is it with you? How is it with your heart? To what or to whom does your heart most truly cling?

God and Wealth

Our story from Luke's gospel is a strange and difficult story. It's about a rich man and his manager. People were coming to the rich man complaining about the manager. "He's squandering your property," they said to the rich man. That will get any rich man's attention. So the rich man set out to investigate the matter. He called the manager to his office. "What is this I hear about you?" said the rich man. "Give me an accounting of your management because you cannot be my manager any longer" (v. 2).

We can just about see the thoughts swirling in the manager's head. He's worried. He's afraid. What to do? That was his primary thought. "What to do to get out of this predicament I'm in? I'm about to lose my job." So the manager came up with a plan; a very clever plan. He had to save his future. He didn't want to dig ditches for a living. He didn't want to become a beggar. Bad options! Then a plan came to him. He wanted to get out of his predicament without cutting himself off from those who had borrowed money from his master. He wanted to do something that would insure he would continue to be welcome in people's homes.

The manager summoned his master's debtors one by one. He asked them, "How much to you owe my master?" The first one quizzed like this said he owed the master a hundred jugs of oil. To this the manager said: "Take your bill, sit down quickly, and make it fifty." The manager was cutting this debtor's debt in half! Not a bad deal for the debtor! The second debtor answered the manager that he owed the master one hundred containers of wheat. "Take your bill and make it eighty," the manager replied (vv. 6-7).

Then the master showed up. We expect him to be furious with the dishonest manager but he's not furious. Rather he commends the manager for acting so shrewdly. The master says, "... for the children of this age are more shrewd in dealing with their own generation than are the children of light." So go on, the master says. Keep it up. "... make friends for yourselves by means of dishonest wealth so that when it is gone, they may welcome you into the eternal homes" (vv. 8-9).

So a dishonest manager is praised by his master. What do we make of this? What's the nice Jesus we know trying to say to us here? It's a difficult story to grasp. Perhaps the best we can do is to understand that Jesus wants us to be prudent and wise as we manage earthly things.

There's more to it than that. Jesus goes on to say that a slave cannot serve two masters. Inevitably the slave will hate one of his masters and love the other one. He will be devoted to one and despise the other. Jesus is clearly saying that we cannot have two masters. His words are very clear. "You cannot serve God and money" (v. 13). That's where this story ends. We can have only one master. We can have only one God. Our heart can truly cling to only one. We cannot serve and love God and wealth or anything else that vies for our faithfulness. Martin Luther once put it this way: "That to which your heart clings and entrusts itself, is, I say, really your god."

Luther's words can serve us as the key to understanding this strange story Jesus tells. Our hearts can truly cling to only one thing and that to which our hearts cling most dearly is surely our god. If we cling most dearly to something that is not God, then clearly, that to which we cling is an idol.

Shadrach, Meshach, and Abednego

Perhaps the most picturesque biblical story of idolatry is told to us in the Old Testament book of Daniel. Shadrach, Meshach, and Abednego: have you heard those names before? Did you sing about them in Sunday school? These three men were close companions of a man called Daniel. In coordination with Daniel these four Jewish men living in exile in Babylon interpreted the mysterious dream of the great king, Nebuchadnezzar. King Nebuchadnezzar rewarded them gloriously. He gave Daniel high honors, great gifts, and made him ruler of the whole province of Babylon. Daniel pleaded with the king to reward his friends as well. So Shadrach, Meshach, and Abednego were also given positions of power in Babylon.

As a result of the good things that came to Nebuchadnezzar because of the dream that Daniel had interpreted for him, Nebuchadnezzar built a large, beautiful image of gold. He called the whole nation for the dedication ceremony of the golden image. When the crowds gathered a herald proclaimed to all who had gathered and told them that when they heard the sound of the horn, pipe, lyre, trigon, harp, bagpipe, and every kind of music, they were to fall down and worship the golden image. The herald spoke words of warning. He said that if anyone does not fall down and worship the golden idol, the person would immediately be thrown into a fiery furnace.

This idol posed a great problem for the Jewish exiles in Babylon. They could not worship a golden idol. Their Ten Commandments strictly prohibit the worship of idols. We remember the words well: "I am the Lord your God, who brought you out of the land of Egypt... you shall have no other gods before me. You shall not make for yourself an idol..." (Exodus 20:2-4). What were the Jewish people in Babylon to do? They would violate the basic foundation of their faith if they worshiped the idol. But if they did not worship the idol, they would be thrown into the fiery furnace. What to do?

Shadrach, Meshach, and Abednego made up their minds to remain faithful to their God. So it was reported to King Nebuchadnezzar that these three Jewish men would not worship the golden idol. The men were brought before the king. Nebuchadnezzar said to them: "Now if you are ready when you hear the sound of the horn, pipe, lyre, trigon, harp, drum, and entire musical ensemble to fall down and worship the statue that I have made, well and good. But if you do not worship, you shall immediately be thrown into a furnace of blazing fire, and who is the god that will deliver you out of my hands?" (Daniel 3:15).

Shadrach, Meshach, and Abednego stood firmly in their faith. They answered Nebuchadnezzar's challenge about what god could deliver them out of his hands. "Our God whom we serve is able to deliver us," they said back to the king "... we will not worship the golden statue that you have set up" (Daniel 3:18).

So the three faithful Jewish men were cast into the fire. The king ordered the heat of the fire to be seven times more than usual. The flame was so hot that it killed the men who threw Shadrach and his friends into the fire! Then the king saw something that frightened him very much. He looked into the fiery flames and saw not three but four men. The appearance of the fourth man, said the king, was like a son of the gods. Nebuchadnezzar was puzzled and frightened by what he saw. So he ordered the three men to be taken out of the fire. Nebuchadnezzar was seemingly converted on the spot. He said: "Blessed be the God of Shadrach, Meshach, and Abednego, who has sent his angel and delivered his servants who trusted in him. They disobeyed the king's command and yielded up their bodies rather than serve and worship any god except their own God" (Daniel 3:28).

Contemporary Idols

Now surely none of us is ever going to be commanded to worship a golden idol lest we be cast into a fiery furnace. The temptations set before us are not of this nature. A group of lay people were asked what they saw as the idols that would pull us away from our fundamental commitment to the God of Jesus Christ. Hear them in no particular order of importance.

One person said that sports had become an idol for many people today. Sports can gobble up our time and leave other commitments behind us. Weekends are committed to the television screen. This is the number one priority.

Another said that wealth is a dangerous modern idol. This is a problem they felt when one was able to get far ahead financially and then forget the people in need. Self-indulgence becomes all consuming. Acquisition is a game without rules. Countless hours can be spent figuring and gaming the financial system for one's gain. It's all about me and my 401K.

Still another felt that personal ambition has become an attractive idol. One covets power, prestige, and influence for oneself. Forget the trials and cares of the rest of the world. I'm all about me! That's my god! In response to this last sentiment one of the members of the group said, "There is only one God and I am not it!"

We could go on listing possible temptations that come our way but this gives us a start as we think about our own lives. Clearly there are many things other than God to which our hearts can cling. Remember what Luther said: "That to which your heart clings and entrusts itself, is, I say, really your god." We each need to search our own hearts to see that to which our hearts most powerfully cling.

Choosing Wisely

Our gospel text from Luke ends with a clear call to discipleship. "You cannot serve God and wealth." You cannot serve God and any other possible idol. That's Jesus' word to us today. His words are a challenge to our idolatrous ways. We can't have it both ways!

The story from the book of Daniel sends pretty much the same message. Shadrach, Meshach, and Abednego would not bow down to Nebuchadnezzar's golden idol. They would not serve the God of Abraham and Isaac and then fall down and worship a golden idol. And into the fiery furnace they went. They chose their own God. They got the furnace. And we find that God did not desert those who chose the God of Israel. God sent an angel and rescued them from the fiery furnace. Nebuchadnezzar had quizzed this trio of Israelites asking them who the god might be who would rescue them from his hands. Nebuchadnezzar found out who that God might be. "Blessed be the God of Shadrach, Meshach, and Abednego, who has sent his angel and delivered his servants who trusted in him," the king confessed, "… there is no other god who is able to deliver in this way" (Daniel 3:28-29).

"That to which your heart clings and entrusts itself, is, I say, really your god." That's what Martin Luther said. Jesus clearly instructs us to understand that our hearts cannot cling to more than one thing. We cannot serve God and wealth or any other tempting idol.

Shadrach, Meshach, and Abednego clearly instruct us that God will not abandon those whose hearts truly cling to God. There is a promise made to each and every one of us in this old story. Our God offers to deliver us from any fiery furnace that threatens our faith in God. Our lives are secure in the loving hands of God.

Let's close with an invitation. I invite you to let your heart truly cling to our Lord and Savior Jesus Christ. That's today's invitation. That's tomorrow's invitation. That's the ongoing invitation of our lives. Cling to Jesus Christ and him alone. No golden idols for us. Our hearts cling to only one reality — the reality of God's love for us in Jesus Christ. Amen.

Proper 21
Pentecost 19
Ordinary Time 26
Luke 16:19-31

Jesus Turns the World Upside Down

> *There was a rich man who was dressed in purple and fine linen and who feasted sumptuously every day. And at his gate lay a poor man named Lazarus, covered with sores, who longed to satisfy his hunger with what fell from the rich man's table; even the dogs would come and lick his sores. The poor man died and was carried away by the angels to be with Abraham. The rich man also died and was buried. In Hades, where he was being tormented, he looked up and saw Abraham far away with Lazarus by his side. He called out, "Father Abraham, have mercy on me, and send Lazarus to dip the tip of his finger in water and cool my tongue; for I am in agony in these flames." But Abraham said, "Child, remember that during your lifetime you received your good things, and Lazarus in like manner evil things; but now he is comforted here, and you are in agony. Besides all this, between you and us a great chasm has been fixed, so that those who might want to pass from here to you cannot do so, and no one can cross from there to us." He said, "Then, father, I beg you to send him to my father's house — for I have five brothers — that he may warn them, so that they will not also come into this place of torment." Abraham replied, "They have Moses and the prophets; they should listen to them." He said, "No, father Abraham; but if someone goes to them from the dead, they will repent." He said to him, "If they do not listen to Moses and the prophets, neither will they be convinced even if someone rises from the dead."* — Luke 16:19-31

An elderly gentleman named Al got the shock of his life in his doctor's office. He had detected a growth under his left cheek and had gone to the doctor to find out what it was. The doctor tried giving him different kinds of pills but nothing worked. Finally, the doctor sent Al to get a biopsy. The results were shocking. He had cancer (mantle cell lymphoma). This type of cancer offered a three- to six-year life possibility. It was said to be incurable.

Al got himself to a cancer doctor right away. The doctor prescribed a series of eight chemotherapy sessions. After four months and six treatments of chemotherapy Al was at his lowest point. The chemotherapy was suspended. Al was in misery. In his misery he determined to try another doctor and off he went to the Mayo Clinic. The doctor assigned to his case was an expert in mantle cell lymphoma. He put Al on a trial drug for chemotherapy. It didn't seem to help much either and was suspended after about four months. Then the doctor prescribed another form of chemotherapy. That's just what Al was trying to avoid! But the new treatments went on over a series of six months.

In the beginning of month nine Al was called in for a CT scan to determine the status of his cancer. He went to the doctor's to view the CT scan with mixed emotions. What if nothing had happened with the treatments? What if the cancer had exploded into different parts of his body? When he got to the doctor's office, the doctor and Al discussed some side effects of the therapy. Finally, Al got to the point. "When do I get to see the pictures?" he asked the doctor. The doctor replied softly: "There is nothing to see." Nothing to see! What did that mean? Then slowly it dawned on Al that there was no cancer to see on the CT scan. For the moment, at least, the cancer was in remission. Al felt deep in his bones that his world had just turned upside down.

Mary's Song

When Mary realized, with the help of an angel, that she was pregnant with the son of God she sang a song. We call it the *Magnificat*. Luke tells of this song at the very beginning of his gospel. The song has many themes that are carried out through stories as Luke tells in his gospel. One of the themes of Mary's *Magnificat* goes like this: "He [God] has brought down the powerful from their thrones, and lifted up the lowly." Reversal! Put down the mighty! Lift up the lowly. It's a theme that sounds again and again in Luke's stories.

Our gospel lesson for today is one of those reversal stories. It's a story of two men. One of the men is very rich. One of the men is very poor. The rich man dressed in the finest clothes of his day. He always looked like a million dollars! One of the occasions that the rich man dressed for was the great banquets he would throw for his friends. There was food galore. The rich man knew how to throw a lavish party!

The second man in Luke's story is a very poor man. His name is Lazarus. Lazarus often laid at the rich man's gate begging for some of the food from the rich man's table. He was poor. He was full of sores. His only friends seemed to be the dogs that came and licked his sores. So, two men: a very rich man, and a very poor man.

Now it happened that the poor man died. To our great surprise we hear from Jesus that angels attended the poor man's death and carried him off to be with Abraham in heaven. We recognize Abraham as the man to whom God spoke God's first great promise to the future people of Israel (Genesis 12:1-3). Then the rich man died and was buried but he did not show up at Abraham's bosom. Not at all! He found himself being tormented in Hades. In his agony he looked up and saw the poor man who had always been at his gate in the company of Abraham! This is really a world turned upside down!

The rich man appealed to Abraham. "Father Abraham," the rich man said, "have mercy on me, and send Lazarus to dip the tip of his finger in water and cool my tongue; for I am in agony in these flames." Abraham astonished the rich man with his answer. "Child, remember that during your lifetime you received your good things, and Lazarus in like manner evil things; but now he is comforted here, and you are in agony" (vv. 24-25).

Abraham goes on to tell the rich man of the great gulf that now separates the two men. Abraham says that the gulf is there to keep the rich man and the poor man separated forever: "... those who might want to pass from here to you cannot do so, and no one can cross from there to us" (v. 26).

The rich man wasn't done with Abraham. He had a special request. He asked Abraham to send the poor man to his home where he had five brothers. Please have the poor man warn my brothers so that they do not end their days as my companions in this world of torment.

Abraham replied that his brothers have Moses and the prophets. His brothers can listen to them! The rich man pleaded on: "No, father Abraham; but if someone goes to them from the dead, they will repent." And then Abraham makes a very strange reply. He says: "If they do not listen to Moses and the prophets, neither will they be convinced even if someone rises from the dead" (v. 30). These are rather shocking words. We, of course, think immediately of Jesus when we hear about one rising from the dead. Does Luke mean to tell us that the Easter message of the resurrection of Jesus has no power? We'll come back to that question later.

What we witness in this story from Luke is part of the fulfillment of Mary's song. God has put down the mighty from their thrones. God has lifted up those of low degree. The God that Mary sang about so magnificently is indeed a God who in Jesus Christ turns the world upside down. The poor man is exalted. The rich man is sent away empty.

Easter

Let's look at one more story from Luke's gospel that is the fulfillment of Mary's song. It's one of the final stories in

Luke's gospel. It's the Easter story. At early dawn of the first day of the week after Jesus had summarily been put to death by the Romans, a band of Jesus' women followers of Jesus showed up at his tomb in order to anoint his body for burial. When they arrived at the tomb they were shocked! The stone had been rolled away from the tomb. They stared into empty space. There was no body there. Jesus was gone!

The women were dumbfounded at the sight. Then suddenly they saw two men in dazzling clothes standing beside them. The women were terrified. They bowed their faces to the ground. The dazzling ones spoke to them: "Why do you look for the living among the dead? He is not here, but has risen" (Luke 24:5).

Can you even begin to put yourself in the place of these women on that first Easter morning? It was shocking. Astonishing! Can such things be? Slowly, catching their wits, they remembered Jesus' words to them that he would be crucified and rise again from the dead. They had thought this was all an idle dream. But, no! It was reality! Jesus had risen from the tomb just as he had promised. Death was destroyed. Jesus had turned the reality of death and the grave upside down.

Then it was the disciples' turn. The women told the disciples what they had seen and heard about Jesus. But the men didn't believe a word of it. It seemed to them to be an idle tale. Later that day two of the disciples were walking toward a village called Emmaus. They were walking and talking about the sad ending of Jesus' life when Jesus showed up on the road walking with them. But the men's eyes were blinded. They didn't recognize Jesus at all. Jesus engaged the men in conversation asking them what they had been talking about. The disciples were astonished at the ignorance of this seeming stranger who had joined them. Didn't he know the things that had taken place in Jerusalem the past few days? Everybody else in town knew what had happened. How could it be that this man hadn't heard the story?

So the disciples told Jesus his own story! There was a prophet named Jesus, mighty in word and deed, and our chief priests and leaders handed him over to the authorities to be killed. So they blabbered on telling Jesus, the risen one they did not recognize, his own story. Finally Jesus stopped them in their storytelling tracks. He said to them, "Oh, how foolish you are, and how slow of heart to believe all that the prophets have declared! Was it not necessary that the Messiah should suffer these things and then enter into his glory?" (Luke 24:25-26). Jesus then proceeded to interpret for the disciples just how their scriptures had pointed to him. Here he was — alive — raised from the dead. Death had been turned upside down. God through his Son Jesus Christ had turned the whole world upside down.

The Turning of the World

Mary sang that it would happen. "God has put down the powerful from their thrones and lifted up the lowly." That is Mary's song. God is in the business of turning the world upside down. In Jesus' story the poor man, Lazarus, went to heaven to live with Abraham. The rich man, however, was cast down into Hades and lived there with no hope.

And then there is Luke's Easter story. A simple man named Jesus was put to death by the established authorities. But God lifted up the lowly one named Jesus. God raised Jesus from the dead to reign with God for all eternity. Just when things looked so very bad for Lazarus and for Jesus, God intervened. God turned the world upside down. God is still turning the world upside down. Jesus might say it this way:

> *I have come from God to turn your world upside down. I have come to you in your world of sin and I offer to forgive you. I turn your sinful world upside down.*

I have come to you in your world filled with evil forces and I conquer those forces. I turn the evil forces that surround you upside down.

I have come to you in your world filled with death and I turn those death forces into life forces. I turn the world of death that haunts you upside down.

I am Jesus sent by God to turn your whole world upside down!

Amen.

**Proper 22
Pentecost 20
Ordinary Time 27
Luke 17:5-10**

Jesus Our Teacher

The apostles said to the Lord, "Increase our faith!" The Lord replied, "If you had faith the size of a mustard seed, you could say to this mulberry tree, 'Be uprooted and planted in the sea,' and it would obey you. Who among you would say to your slave who has just come in from plowing or tending sheep in the field, 'Come here at once and take your place at the table'? Would you not rather say to him, 'Prepare supper for me, put on your apron and serve me while I eat and drink; later you may eat and drink'? Do you thank the slave for doing what was commanded? So you also, when you have done all that you were ordered to do, say, 'We are worthless slaves; we have done only what we ought to have done!' " — Luke 17:5-10

We know Jesus as our savior from human sin. We know Jesus as the one who conquered death and the grave on Easter morning promising us eternal life. We know Jesus as the one sent from God to defeat the evil powers that threaten our human lives. Jesus as savior. Jesus as the risen one. Jesus as the one who defeats evil power. That's the Jesus we know and love. In our text for today we see Jesus in a different role. Here we see Jesus as teacher!

Jesus has some interesting things to teach us in this scripture reading. With these words we come to the end of an important section of Luke's gospel. From Luke 15:1 through Luke 17:10 Jesus offers all kinds of instruction for Christian living. We've heard these stories in previous weeks: the story of the prodigal son and the story of the rich man and Lazarus and others. We have come to an end of this section of Jesus' teaching before Jesus sets his face for his final days in Jerusalem.

Temptation

The story assigned for today is a short section from Luke 17:5-10. We will add verses 1-4 to our consideration for these verses are an integral part of Jesus' teaching as he prepares to head for his final days in Jerusalem. These ten verses give us four aspects of how God's grace is to work itself out in our lives. God's love for us sinful human beings is the heart of the matter here.

Jesus said to his disciples, "Occasions for stumbling are bound to come, but woe to anyone by whom they come!" (17:1). In other translations the word "temptation" is used in place of "occasions for stumbling." Temptations will come! That's Jesus' word, and we know deep in our bones that Jesus is "right on" with his words. Temptations do come to us. They come all the time. They come every day. We are tempted to put our own needs and desires above all else. We are tempted most fundamentally to put ourselves at the center of our universe.

According to the story of Adam and Eve, the primal temptation of human beings is to wish to be like God! That was the temptation Satan put to Eve in Genesis 3. Satan wanted Eve to eat of the fruit of the tree in the midst of the garden. Eve said, "No. God told us not to eat of the fruit of that tree or we would die." "No, no, no," said Satan. "You won't die. On the contrary, if you eat of the tree you will be like God." Imagine that: to be like God! Eve bit on that temptation immediately. Who wouldn't want to be like God? That's the fundamental temptation of each and every one of us. Let me be the center of the universe. Let the world revolve around me. Let me have everything I want.

I think every one of us knows deep in our bones that this is, indeed, our most fundamental temptation in life. We want to be godlike. We want to be the center of our own universe. This just might be our fundamental human problem. In our story from Luke, however, Jesus does not scold or blame us for our self-centered ways. This is very surprising. "Occasions for stumbling are bound to come," Jesus says. But he does not point the finger of blame at us. He points his finger of blame at those who do the tempting. "It would be better for you (the tempter) if a millstone were hung around your neck and you were thrown into the sea than for you to cause one of these little ones to stumble" (17:2).

Temptations may come from people all around us. We all know that it is true and the temptations will keep coming. That's just the way life is. But we don't need to feel guilty about this reality. It's the way life is. Jesus is on our side to help us find our way through all the temptations of life. God's grace and mercy are on our side in this whole matter of sin and temptation. Thanks be to God.

Forgiveness

Jesus goes on with his dialogue to give us additional advice about temptation and forgiveness. How are we to relate to those who bring temptation into our lives? We know this happens all the time. How should we react to such people? Jesus' first word here is that we should rebuke those who put temptation in our path. Isn't that good advice? There are people we would like to rebuke.

But Jesus has more to say on this subject. Jesus is not just asking us to judge those who tempt us. He is also urging us to forgive such people when they repent of their tempting ways. "If there is repentance, you must forgive!" That's Jesus' word for us. And we are called to forgive others not just once! "… if the same person sins against you seven times a day, and turns back to you seven times and says, 'I repent,' you must forgive" (17:4).

Our Christian lives, created as they are by God's forgiveness of our sinfulness, are to be lives marked by the amazing ability to forgive those who trespass against us. Even if they sin against us seven times. Even if it never seems to stop. Christians are forgiven people. Forgiven people are forgiving people. "You must forgive," Jesus says. Not to forgive others is a violation of the grace of God by which we have our lives as Christians. When we are unwilling to forgive others, we forget that our lives as Christians are grounded in the forgiving grace of God. Forgiven people are forgiving people! God's loving forgiveness for us never ends. Our forgiveness of others should never end as well.

Faith

Perhaps the disciples were thrown off balance by Jesus' words about forgiving others. They knew how hard it is to carry that out in actual human living. So they ask Jesus to increase their faith. "The apostles said to the Lord, 'Increase our faith!' " (v. 5). Increase our faith! That's a good prayer. Wouldn't we all like to pray that prayer to God? "Please God, increase my faith!" We know we are called upon to put our faith ultimately in Jesus Christ. But there are so many obstacles in our way! We are tempted, instead, to put our faith in ourselves.

We are tempted, for example, to put our faith in our strength of intelligence. I can figure this life thing out! I know best how to live my life. I don't need any help in this matter. I am self-sufficient. I can be my own savior. I can make up my own religion. People are doing that by the thousands. They just make up what it is they want to believe is the ultimate focus of human life. This is the sin of pride run amuck. We don't know what is best for ourselves. We cannot be god!

We might choose to center our own lives in the accumulation of worldly goods. We work hard to get a job that will sustain us. We make wise investments. We seek to forge long-range plans for our retirement. We can do this by ourselves. We believe in ourselves.

In this text we are called instead to put our faith in Jesus. The disciples, therefore, asked Jesus to increase their faith so that they might live out the fullness of their calling. The disciples must have been thinking that if they only had more faith in Jesus their lives would be fine. We might think like that as well. If I could just get my faith focused squarely in Jesus, then my life would be so much better. Increase my faith, Jesus! Help me out here. We just need more faith. We just need our faith to be stronger.

But Jesus won't go there! He didn't increase the disciple's faith. Rather he spoke a simple parable to them. Jesus said to them, "If you had faith the size of a mustard seed, you could say to this mulberry tree, 'Be uprooted and planted in the sea,' and it would obey you" (v. 6). In other words, Jesus tells the disciples and tells us as well that we don't need more faith. Our little faith will do! The mustard seed is supposedly the smallest thing on earth. Yet Jesus can say faith that is as small as the smallest thing on earth is quite sufficient for our lives! That's astonishing! How can that be? You mean we don't need more faith? Jesus says, "No!" we don't need more faith. Faith the size of a mustard seed will be able to do great things.

Jesus' answer to the disciples' request for an increase of faith is quite surprising. It is also very comforting! Evidently we don't need to find countless ways to increase our faith. Our little faith will do. The little faith we have can do wonders.

Vocation

The final verses of our text lead us to the realm of Christian vocation. Jesus has just established that faith the size of a mustard seed can do great things. In these verses Jesus makes it clear that living lives of Christian service is done for the neighbor and not for ourselves. There is no room for boasting in the Christian life!

Jesus challenges his disciples with a story about a slave who has just come in the house from plowing or tending sheep in a field. He wonders which of the disciples would reward such a servant for doing his duty. Would you say to the servant: "Come here at once and take your place at the table?" In other words, Jesus is asking his disciples if they would reward a servant with a great feast just because he did his job.

Jesus goes on to say that the master of the servant should say: "Prepare supper for me, put on your apron and serve me while I eat and drink; later you may eat and drink" (v. 8). Jesus then makes his point abundantly clear: "Do you thank the slave for doing what was commanded?" (v. 9) he asks the disciples. The answer to Jesus' question is, "No." You don't thank the slave for doing what he is supposed to be doing. Then Jesus comes to the point: "So you also, when you have done all that you were ordered to do, say, 'We are worthless slaves; we have done only what we ought to have done' " (v. 10).

Jesus' story could be heard as a story about Christian vocation. Martin Luther taught that every legitimate vocation is an arena of priestly service. In Luther's time it was thought that only religiously trained people did religious service. Luther turned that idea upside down. According to Luther all baptized persons were ordained, so to speak, to live lives of priestly or spiritual service to their fellow humans.

We live out our priestly calling when we give our lives to others. We serve God when we are faithful spouses. We serve God when we care well for our children. We serve God when we are involved in community service. We serve God when we are active citizens. The list could go on and on. God calls us to simple things. God calls us to love our neighbor wherever we encounter them.

According to Jesus' story there is to be no great reward for serving our neighbor in our various vocations. The servant in Jesus' story did not get a special supper for doing his job! When we serve our neighbor, wherever we find them, we have only done what we ought to have done! The service we render is the reward we receive. There will be no bonuses. There will be no special awards. There will be no certificates of greatness. We are simply called to do what we ought to have done as Christian people. That's how Jesus understands our way of life in this world.

Of course, we know that there are great rewards for those who serve others faithfully in their vocations. There is the gratitude we receive from those we serve. There is the deep satisfaction in a job well done that lifts up our fellow human beings. And there is an eternal reward as well. Doing what we ought to have done in the name of Jesus Christ culminates in life and in a new heaven and a new earth. We shouldn't be surprised if that life also consists of service done on behalf of others!

Proclamation

We said at the outset that God's love for us is the real heart of the matter in this text from Luke's gospel. God's love is manifested clearly in each of the stories in his teaching of the disciples. First, there is the matter of temptation. Jesus would say to us: "I, too, faced temptation and I overcame its power. I will walk with you in life and be present for you in every temptation that you face."

Second, there is the matter of forgiveness. Jesus says to us: "When you repent of your sins I hear you. I will always embrace you with my forgiving love."

Third, we heard of faith the size of a mustard seed. "I see your little faith," Jesus says to us, "I see your little faith and I promise that you can move mountains with your little faith."

Fourth, we heard about vocation. Jesus says to us: "I have called you to serve me as a priest to others in all aspects of your life. I will give you the strength you need to love others as I have loved you." Amen.

If You Like This Book...

Richard Jensen has also written **Preaching Matthew's Gospel** (978-0-7880-1221-1) (printed book $22.95, e-book $9.95), **Preaching Luke's Gospel** (978-0-7880-1110-8-X) (printed book $24.95, e-book $19.95), **Preaching Mark's Gospel** (978-0-7880-0833-7) (printed book $18.95, e-book $9.95), **Lectionary Tales for the Pulpit,** Cycle C (978-0-7880-0081-2) (printed book $15.94, e-book $9.95) **Thinking In Story** (978-1-55673-573-8) (printed book $13.95, e-book $9.95).

Other Cycle C Pentecost (Middle Third) Lectionary Titles...

What if What They Say Is True?
John Wurster
978-0-7880-1722-3
printed book $12.95 / e-book $9.95

Topsy-Turvy Living in the Biblical World
Thomas Renquist
978-0-7880-1737-7
printed book $12.95 / e-book $9.95

contact CSS Publishing Company, Inc.
www.csspub.com   **800-241-4056**

Prices are subject to change without notice.

All Stirred Up
Richard Patt
978-0-7880-1040-8
printed book $12.95 / e-book $9.95

Lord, Send the Wind
James McLemore
978-0-7880-1039-2
printed book $12.95 / e-book $9.95

Troubled Journey
John Lynch
978-0-7880-0015-7
printed book $12.95 / e-book $9.95

Summer Fruit
Richard Sheffield
978-0-7880-0040-9
printed book $12.95 / e-book $9.95

contact CSS Publishing Company, Inc.
www.csspub.com   800-241-4056

Prices are subject to change without notice.

www.ingramcontent.com/pod-product-compliance
Lightning Source LLC
Chambersburg PA
CBHW071732040426
42446CB00011B/2330